编审委员会

主　任　　侯建国

副主任　　窦贤康　　陈初升
　　　　　　　张淑林　　朱长飞

委　员（按姓氏笔画排序）

方兆本	史济怀	古继宝	伍小平
刘　斌	刘万东	朱长飞	孙立广
汤书昆	向守平	李曙光	苏　淳
陆夕云	杨金龙	张淑林	陈发来
陈华平	陈初升	陈国良	陈晓非
周学海	胡化凯	胡友秋	俞书勤
侯建国	施蕴渝	郭光灿	郭庆祥
奚宏生	钱逸泰	徐善驾	盛六四
龚兴龙	程福臻	蒋　一	窦贤康
褚家如	滕脉坤	霍剑青	

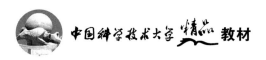

Original English Reading

原生态英语阅读

主　编　徐守平

参编人员　（按姓氏笔画排序）

丁菲菲　马仁蓉　任爱军　许振宇
何朝阳　邹红云　陈　静　陈馥梅
徐守平　斯　骏　管　琛　薛光荣

中国科学技术大学出版社

内 容 简 介

本书以弘扬人文精神、培养学生的英语应用能力为宗旨,书中的文章均选自国外的图书和报刊,以论述文、说明文为主,未做改写、简化,以期培养学生直接阅读原生态英语的能力。本书共14个单元,每个单元后附有与该单元内容相关的作文题,希望读者通过阅读、思辨、模仿提高论述文、说明文的写作能力。

本书适合希望提高英语读、写能力的大学生阅读,也可作为四六级英语考试、研究生英语入学考试、托福、GRE备考的辅助教材。

图书在版编目(CIP)数据

原生态英语阅读/徐守平主编. —合肥:中国科学技术大学出版社,2018.8(2019.9重印)

(中国科学技术大学精品教材)

安徽省"十三五"重点出版物出版规划项目

ISBN 978-7-312-04485-4

Ⅰ. 原… Ⅱ. 徐… Ⅲ. 英语—阅读教学—自学参考资料 Ⅳ. H319.4

中国版本图书馆 CIP 数据核字(2018)第 153450 号

出版	中国科学技术大学出版社 安徽省合肥市金寨路96号,230026 http://press.ustc.edu.cn https://zgkxjsdxcbs.tmall.com
印刷	安徽国文彩印有限公司
发行	中国科学技术大学出版社
经销	全国新华书店
开本	710 mm×1000 mm 1/16
插页	2
印张	15.5
字数	270 千
版次	2018 年 8 月第 1 版
印次	2019 年 9 月第 2 次印刷
定价	36.00 元

Preface
总　　序

2008年,为庆祝中国科学技术大学建校五十周年,反映建校以来的办学理念和特色,集中展示教材建设的成果,学校决定组织编写出版代表中国科学技术大学教学水平的精品教材系列。在各方的共同努力下,共组织选题281种,经过多轮、严格的评审,最后确定50种入选精品教材系列。

五十周年校庆精品教材系列于2008年9月纪念建校五十周年之际陆续出版,共出书50种,在学生、教师、校友以及高校同行中引起了很好的反响,并整体进入国家新闻出版总署的"十一五"国家重点图书出版规划。为继续鼓励教师积极开展教学研究与教学建设,结合自己的教学与科研积累编写高水平的教材,学校决定,将精品教材出版作为常规工作,以《中国科学技术大学精品教材》系列的形式长期出版,并设立专项基金给予支持。国家新闻出版总署也将该精品教材系列继续列入"十二五"国家重点图书出版规划。

1958年学校成立之时,教员大部分来自中国科学院的各个研究所。作为各个研究所的科研人员,他们到学校后保持了教学的同时又作研究的传统。同时,根据"全院办校,所系结合"的原则,科学院各个研究所在科研第一线工作的杰出科学家也参与学校的教学,为本科生授课,将最新的科研成果融入到教学中。虽然现在外界环境和内在条件都发生了很大变化,但学校以教学为主、教学与科研相结合的方针没有变。正因为坚持了科学与技术相结合、理论与实践相结合、教学与科研相结合的方针,并形成了优良的传统,才培养出了一批又一批高质量的人才。

学校非常重视基础课和专业基础课教学的传统,也是她特别成功的原因之一。当今社会,科技发展突飞猛进、科技成果日新月异,没有扎实的基础知识,很难在科学技术研究中作出重大贡献。建校之初,华罗庚、吴有训、严济慈等老一辈科学家、教育家就身体力行,亲自为本科生讲授基础课。他们以渊博的学识、精湛的讲课艺术、高尚的师德,带出一批又一批杰出的年轻教员,培养了一届又一届优秀学生。入选精品教材系列的绝大部分是基础课或专业基础课的教材,其作者大多直接或间接受到过这些老一辈科学家、教育家的教诲和影响,因此在教材中也贯穿着这些先辈的教育教学理念与科学探索精神。

改革开放之初,学校最先选派青年骨干教师赴西方国家交流、学习,他们在带回先进科学技术的同时,也把西方先进的教育理念、教学方法、教学内容等带回到中国科学技术大学,并以极大的热情进行教学实践,使"科学与技术相结合、理论与实践相结合、教学与科研相结合"的方针得到进一步深化,取得了非常好的效果,培养的学生得到全社会的认可。这些教学改革影响深远,直到今天仍然受到学生的欢迎,并辐射到其他高校。在入选的精品教材中,这种理念与尝试也都有充分的体现。

中国科学技术大学自建校以来就形成的又一传统是根据学生的特点,用创新的精神编写教材。进入我校学习的都是基础扎实、学业优秀、求知欲强、勇于探索和追求的学生,针对他们的具体情况编写教材,才能更加有利于培养他们的创新精神。教师们坚持教学与科研的结合,根据自己的科研体会,借鉴目前国外相关专业有关课程的经验,注意理论与实际应用的结合,基础知识与最新发展的结合,课堂教学与课外实践的结合,精心组织材料、认真编写教材,使学生在掌握扎实的理论基础的同时,了解最新的研究方法,掌握实际应用的技术。

入选的这些精品教材,既是教学一线教师长期教学积累的成果,也是学校教学传统的体现,反映了中国科学技术大学的教学理念、教学特色和教学改革成果。希望该精品教材系列的出版,能对我们继续探索科教紧密结合培养拔尖创新人才,进一步提高教育教学质量有所帮助,为高等教育事业作出我们的贡献。

侯建国

中国科学院院士
第三世界科学院院士

Foreword
前　　言

　　本书是为了满足中国科学技术大学(简称"中国科大")本科英语读写课程的教学需求而编写的。大学英语教学应该充分考虑学生的特点,因材施教。中国科大本科生的英语起点较高,对英语学习的要求和目的也有所不同。在实际教学过程中,我们发现,中国科大本科生以往接触的英语阅读材料多为记叙文,而且文章在难度和词汇量方面都有人为的控制,这种控制在一定的阶段是必要的,但对于中国一流大学的本科生来说,这种控制不利于学生日后的学习和工作。中国科大本科生毕业后主要有三个去向:出国留学、国内深造和就业创业。基于这三个去向,我们认为学生需要阅读更多的论述文和说明文,需要了解在讨论某些学术性较强的话题时如何组织思想、选择恰当的语言,需要有能力直接阅读原生态的英语,习惯于阅读难度相当于一线英语杂志上的文章,并需要借助于阅读提高自己论述文和说明文的写作能力。

　　每一种语言都有自己独特的表达定式,深受语言文化背景的影响。读写课程教学不仅应该着眼于语言技能,而且应该重视文化背景对语言学习的作用。本书共分14个单元,从不同的角度反映英语文化的特点,让学生浸入含有不同文化信息的语言环境,帮助学生获得较强的语言运用能力,以满足日常的文化交际需求。

　　同时,我们意识到自主学习对提高学生的英语应用能力至关重要。在实际教学中,我们鼓励学生多读课外书,但由于课外书种类繁多,在课堂上无法检查、督促,因此我们在编写本书时,每个单元都刻意留下一两篇文章,要求学生自学,然后教师在课堂上检查,并在期中、期末考试中以适当的题型考查学生课外阅读的内容,以有效地增加学生的阅读量。

　　本书为中国科大教改后的英语读写教学量身定做,与教改配套。书中的文章均选自国外的图书和报刊,未做改写、简化,风格多样,文字优美,视角独特,语言表述恣意纵横,具有较强的文化冲击力。通过接触原生态英语,学生可以为后续学习、工作打好英语读写基础。书中每个单元都配有阅读、写作练习,每篇文章有五个标注了下划线的句子,可作为翻译练习。全书的课文和练习设计具有较强的针对性,集中国科大外语系读写组全体教员的智慧,适合课堂教学。

  在本书编写、试用过程中,我们得到了中国科大教务处的大力支持,同时也得到了孙蓝教授、崔海建教授的具体帮助,在此一并表示感谢。

编 者

2018 年 1 月

Contents
目　　录

Preface ·· (ⅰ)

Foreword ·· (ⅲ)

Unit One　New Trends ··· (1)

  1. "Mystery Meat" Takes on a Whole New Meaning ················ (1)

  2. Friends? Who Needs Them ··· (8)

  3. The End of the Full-Time Salaried Job ······························ (14)

Unit Two　Individual Growth ·· (21)

  1. The Essence of Charm ··· (21)

  2. Average Is Over ··· (29)

  3. Are You a Striver, Slacker or Fantasist? ···························· (35)

Unit Three　Youth Today ·· (40)

  1. How Those Spoiled Millennials Will Make the Workplace Better for Everyone ··· (40)

  2. Harvard Cheating Scandal: Is Academic Dishonesty on the Rise? ·· (47)

Unit Four　Social Concerns ··· (53)

  1. The Price of Marriage in China ······································· (53)

  2. Will There Be Any Nature Left? ····································· (61)

3. A World Without Books? ……………………………………………… (67)

Unit Five Business and Market (71)
1. Things Go Better with Quark? ……………………………………… (71)
2. What Is a Bank? ……………………………………………………… (78)
3. Why We're Spending So Much on Botox, Makeup and Facelifts ………… (84)

Unit Six Technology Development (90)
1. Human Gait Could Soon Power Portable Electronics ……………… (90)
2. How Solar Can Save India's Farmers ……………………………… (95)
3. Is the Mobile Phone a Blessing or a Curse? ……………………… (103)

Unit Seven Medical World (107)
1. Why We Should Study Cancer Like We Study Ecosystems ………… (107)
2. Three Ways Video Games Can Improve Health Care ……………… (114)
3. Yes, Don't Impede Medical Progress ……………………………… (121)

Unit Eight Coping Strategies (128)
1. Water Damage ………………………………………………………… (128)
2. How to Write ………………………………………………………… (134)

Unit Nine Surviving Skills (142)
1. Survival of the Biggest ……………………………………………… (142)
2. How Reading Good Works Makes Us More Effective? …………… (148)

Unit Ten Education Issues (152)
1. The Trouble with Online Education ………………………………… (152)
2. Really Useful Schooling ……………………………………………… (160)

Unit Eleven Culture Studies (165)
1. *Lost in Thailand*: Did China's Comedy Hit Get Lost in Translation?
   ……………………………………………………………………… (165)
2. Preserve the Country's Own Culture ……………………………… (172)

Unit Twelve New Insight (178)
1. Why Waiting Is Torture ……………………………………………… (178)

2. Pathways Seen For Acquiring Languages ········· (186)

Unit Thirteen Personality and Character ················· (194)

1. The Ungrateful President ······················· (194)

2. The Five Images of Love ························ (201)

3. Embracing the Mystery of Einstein ············· (210)

Unit Fourteen New Horizon ······························· (218)

1. What If Women Ruled the World? ··············· (218)

2. The Soul of the Olympics ························ (225)

3. We Still Need Information Stored in Our Heads Not "in the Cloud"

··· (232)

Key to Comprehension Questions ························ (238)

Unit One New Trends

1. "Mystery Meat[1]" Takes on a Whole New Meaning

By Christie Wilcox[2]

1   In case you didn't hear, the big news in the food industry this week is the fact that — gasp — horsemeat has been detected in Burger King burgers and Ikea's Swedish meatballs. Noses worldwide are turning up in disgust at the use of such crude ingredients in ground beef products.

2   There's no doubt that a good part of the fuss is that, for some of the Western world, horsemeat is taboo. Many people have an immediate, visceral reaction to the notion of eating horse, just like Americans generally react strongly to the idea of eating dogs. While our preferences are culturally rooted, the recent labeling exposures don't just offend our palates. ① As consumers, we rely on retailers and restaurants to give us accurate information about which foods we are buying — whether it be to avoid allergies, follow religious preferences, choose more sustainable options, or count calories. Now, DNA barcoding is exposing just how often we are duped.

3   Labeling isn't a European problem. In South Africa, game is a popular alternative to beef, with over 2.5 million hectares of land dedicated to farming a wide variety of wild meats. But a study published in Investigative Genetics

today found that more than 3/4 of the game samples they tested were not the animal they said they were. Cuts labeled as wild game species were identified as horse, kangaroo, pork, lamb, and a suite of African animals not on the labels. The most prevalent substitution occurred for products labeled kudu (92 percent were mislabeled). A different South African study tells a similar story. ② <u>A study of beef products in South Africa published earlier this week found that 68% of samples contained species not declared in the product label, including donkey, buffalo, goat and pork, and almost a third of the products contained soy and gluten, even though the labels didn't tell the consumer that.</u> But, they didn't find any horsemeat in their beef.

4   In the U.S., studies have found that more than 1/3 of all U.S. fish are mislabeled. A recent Oceana report found that 39 percent of fish sold in NY grocery stores, fish markets and sushi restaurants were not the fish they claimed to be, building on their earlier findings of in Boston (48 percent), Los Angeles (55 percent), and Miami (31 percent). Every single one of the 16 sushi restaurants tested sold mislabeled fish. Some species were substituted more often — 69 percent of the tuna sold wasn't tuna, and thirteen different species were sold falsely under the label "red snapper". But perhaps the worst part was that 94 percent of white tuna sold was actually escolar, a fish species known to cause poisoning. While the world is fretting about horses, I'd rather eat a little horsemeat than diarrhea-inducing escolar any day.

5   Why does it seem so hard for the world to correctly label the species in our stores? Part of the problem is that there is high economic incentive to lie. Species that are worth top dollar are particularly lucrative to forge. Until now, exposing such fraud has been difficult, as many species look the same once they're ground, cut or filleted. But now, we can test foods on the genetic level, allowing us to identify all species present. ③ <u>Given these frauds have real financial, religious, ethical and public health ramifications, it seems past time that genetic testing become a constant part of the regulatory process.</u>

6   Actually enacting such legislation, however, has proven difficult. In the

U.K., the Food Standards Authority was quick to commission genetic testing after the scandal hit, but beforehand, testing had been declining for years. In the U.S., the USDA only genetically tests meat when there is a reason to suspect horseplay, and despite our clear fish labeling problem, no action was taken when *the Safety And Fraud Enforcement for Seafood (SAFE Seafood) Act* was introduced last year. If we want to improve labeling, we need to push our governments and tell them that genetic testing is non-negotiable.

7 Perhaps, though, it is also time to look inward and reflect on our own cultural biases. What makes a cow so much better to eat than a horse, anyway? Why not make burgers out of insects? ④ In a world where fishery after fishery collapses under our demand and livestock threatens our land, air and water resources, perhaps we need to diversify our idea of what is fit for our plates, and ultimately seek to minimize our ecological footprint by any food necessary. ⑤ If there is anything that our labeling failures have exposed, it is the need to closely examine the animals we consume and the ways we catch or farm them to determine the best ones for us, both in terms of nutrition and by measures of sustainability.

(From *Discover*, February 28, 2013)

Notes

[1] **Mystery Meat**: A disparaging term for meat products, typically ground or otherwise processed, such as burger patties, chicken nuggets, steaks, sausages, or hot dogs, that have an unidentifiable source. Most often the term is used in reference to food served in institutional cafeterias, such as prison food or an American public school lunch. The term is also sometimes applied to meat products where the species from which the meat has come from is known (e. g., cow or pig), but the cuts of meat (i. e., the parts of the animal) used are unknown. This is often the case where the cuts of meat used include offal and

mechanically separated meat, where explicitly stating the type of meat used might diminish the perceived palatability of the product to some consumers.

[2] Christie Wilcox: PhD, an award-winning science writer with a passion for telling life's most compelling biological stories. Her first nonfiction book, *Venomous*, hit shelves in August 2016, and has garnered widespread acclaim, including coveted spots on the list of "Best Science Books of 2016" from Amazon and Smithsonian Magazine.

Words and Phrases

gasp /gɑːsp/ *v.*
to take a quick deep breath with your mouth open, especially because you are surprise or in pain （尤指惊讶或疼痛时的）倒吸气

grind /graɪnd/ *v.*
to break or crush sth. into very small pieces between two hard surfaces or using a special machine 磨碎

visceral /ˈvɪsərəl/ *adj.*
relating to the viscera 内脏的

palate /ˈpælət/ *n.*
the ability to recognize and/or enjoy good food and drink 味觉；鉴赏力

allergy /ˈælədʒɪ/ *n.*
a medical condition that causes you to react badly or feel ill/sick when you eat or touch a particular substance 过敏反应

calorie /ˈkæləri/ *n.*
a unit for measuring how much energy food will produce 卡路里（热量单位）

barcode /ˈbɑːˈkəʊd/ *n.*
a pattern of thick and thin lines that is printed on things you buy (It contains information that a computer can read.) 条码

hectare /ˈhekteə(r)/ *n.*
a unit for measuring an area of land 公顷

kudu /ˈkudu/ *n.*
a large greyish or brownish African antelope with white stripes on its sides 捻角羚

gluten /ˈgluːtn/ *n.*
a sticky substance that is a mixture of tow proteins and is left when starch is removed from flavor, especially wheat flour 面筋

sushi /ˈsuːʃɪ/ *n.*
a Japanese dish of small cakes of cold cooked rice, flavored with vinegar and served with raw fish, etc. on top 寿司

tuna /ˈtjuːnə/ *n.*
a large sea fish that is used for food 金枪鱼

snapper /ˈsnæpə/ *n.*
a fish that lives in warm seas and is used for food 鲷鱼

escolar /ˌeskəˈlɑː/ *n.*
a fish that lives in the tropical area of the Atlantic Ocean 玉梭鱼

diarrhea /ˌdaɪəˈrɪə/ *n.*
an illness in which waste matter is emptied from the bowels much more frequently than normal, and in liquid form 腹泻

induce /ɪnˈdjuːs/ *v.*
to cause sth. 引起；导致

incentive /ɪnˈsentɪv/ *n.*
something that encourages you to do sth. 激励；刺激

lucrative /ˈluːkrətɪv/ *adj.*
producing a large amount of money 赚钱的

fillet /ˈfɪlɪt/ *v.*
to cut fish or meat into fillets 把（鱼、肉）切成条

ramification /ˌræmɪfɪˈkeɪʃn/ *n.*
one of the large number of complicated and unexpected results that follow an action or a decision 结果；后果

horseplay /ˈhɔːspleɪ/ *n.*

rough noisy play in which people push or hit each other 恶作剧

bias /ˈbaɪəs/ *n.*

a strong feeling in favor of or against one group of people, or one side in an argument, often not based on fair judgement 偏见

fishery /ˈfɪʃərɪ/ *n.*

a part of the sea or a river where fish are caught in large quantities 渔场

diversify /daɪˈvɜːsɪfaɪ/ *v.*

to change or make sth. change so that there is greater variety 使多样化

nutrition /njuˈtrɪʃən/ *n.*

the process by which living things receive the food necessary for them to grow and be healthy 营养

a suite of

a set of 一套

fret about

to be worried or unhappy and not able to relax 苦恼

Reading Comprehension Questions

1. What may be the implication of the word "crude" mentioned in paragraph 1? _____

    (A) Horsemeat is not well processed.

    (B) Horsemeat is offensive to our palate.

    (C) Horsemeat is less nutritious than beef.

    (D) Horsemeat is likely to cause poisoning.

2. The word "taboo" (line 2, paragraph 2) most probably means _____.

    (A) a disease   (B) an evil

    (C) a ban   (D) an incident

3. What is the labeling problem in South Africa? _____

(A) Horsemeat has been detected in their beef.

(B) Beef products contained species not declared in the product label.

(C) Game is a popular alternative to beef.

(D) Fish sold in sushi restaurants were not the fish they claimed to be.

4. What has made it possible for us to identify all species present? _____

    (A) Legislation.   (B) High economic incentive.

    (C) Genetic testing.   (D) Exposing frauds.

5. The last paragraph seems to support that _____ .

    (A) we should choose not to eat meat to guarantee the sustainability of our ecological system

    (B) we should abandon our own culture to preserve our land, air and water resources

    (C) we should change our eating habit to seek to minimize our ecological footprint by any food necessary

    (D) we should closely examine the animals we consume to ensure they are safe and nutritious

(选文、注释:陈静)

2. Friends? Who Needs Them

By Jacob Aron

1   You've set your Facebook account to "friends only", your Tweets are protected and you wouldn't dream of setting a virtual foot near location-sharing services like Foursquare[1]— in other words, you can feel pretty safe online, right? Wrong. We all unwittingly leak vital information through friends.

2   "You can actually infer a lot of things about people, even though they are pretty careful about how they manage their online behaviour," says Adam Sadilek of the University of Rochester in New York. He has developed a system for predicting a Twitter user's location by looking at where their friends are. The tool can correctly place a user within a 100-metre radius with up to 85 percent accuracy.

3   Sadilek and colleagues turn their target's social network into a predictive model called a dynamic Bayesian network[2]. ① <u>At each point in time, the nodes in the target person's network consist of their friends' locations, day of the week and the time, and information from these nodes determines the target's most likely location.</u> Sadilek can also feed in any existing information about the person's whereabouts to help improve the model's accuracy.

4   The team tested their model on over 4 million tweets from users in Los Angeles and New York City, who had location data enabled. They found a couple of weeks of location data on an individual, combined with location data from their two most sharing friends, is enough to place that person with a 100-metre radius with 77 percent accuracy. That rises to nearly 85 percent when you combine information from nine friends. Even someone who has never shared their location can be pinpointed with 47 percent accuracy from information available from two friends, rising to 57 percent with nine.

5   ② Once the model has a good idea of where some people are, it can use this data to predict who their friends are, and then use that social network to pinpoint the whereabouts of even more people.

6   "You can imagine looping this process over and over," says Sadilek, potentially allowing the model to make predictions about every user on Twitter. Privacy advocates may recoil in horror, but Sadilek claims this knowledge could have benefits. It could help identify people who might spread infectious diseases or contact friends nearby to prevent suicide attempts. He will present the work at the Web Search and Data Mining conference in Seattle next month.

7   It is not just Twitter contacts who compromise your privacy. Facebook friends who share too much could help someone access your account. Last year Facebook rolled out a new "social authentication" system designed to block suspicious logins, but computer scientist Hyoungshick Kim and colleagues at the University of Cambridge have discovered some flaws.

8   Suppose you normally access Facebook in London, but one day Facebook sees a login from Australia. You might be on holiday, but it is also possible a hacker has got hold of your password, so Facebook's social authentication system blocks these logins unless you can identify photos of your friends.

9   It seems secure, but Kim points out it only protects you against strangers — a jealous spouse would easily be able to identify mutual friends, for example. Kim's research shows that using photos from non-overlapping communities could prevent this, but that is no good if your friends share their photos publicly, as many people on Facebook do. A determined person could easily gather such photos to create a database of your friend's faces, then use facial recognition software to identify the social authentication photos.

10   ③ Kim suggests that indiscrete friends should be removed from the social authentication system, but even that wouldn't help a specific group of social networkers: celebrities, whose friends are likely to be recognizable. Kim will present the work at the Financial Cryptography and Data Security conference on the island of Bonaire in the Caribbean next month.

11   Even with your friends under control, a software bug could still expose your private data as Facebook CEO Mark Zuckerberg himself found out recently when a glitch revealed his photos to the world. To solve this, researchers at the Massachusetts Institute of Technology have come up with a new programming language called Jeeves that automatically enforces privacy policies.

12   ④ <u>Programmers have to explicitly ensure data flowing through their software obeys necessary privacy policies, but it is easy to slip up and let information leak out.</u> Jeeves solves that by substituting the value of variables with the software depending on who the user is. For example, say Alice posts a message but doesn't want anyone but herself to see who wrote it. The programmer can use the variable "author" without worrying what the user sees — when the software runs, Jeeves ensures Alice will see her own name, but everyone else logging in will see "Anonymous".

13   Jean Yang, who helped develop Jeeves, says ⑤ <u>the new language lets a programmer delegate privacy responsibilities and concentrate on the actual function of their code, much like a party host might entrust their butler with ensuring the needs of each guest are met so they can spend more time socializing.</u>

(From *New Scientist*, January 28, 2012)

Notes

[1] **Foursquare**: Until late July 2014, Foursquare featured a social networking layer that enabled a user to share their location with friends, via the "check in" — a user would manually tell the application when they were at a particular location using a mobile website, text messaging, or a device-specific application by selecting from a list of venues the application locates nearby.

[2] **Bayesian Network**: belief network, Bayes(ian) model or probabilistic directed acyclic graphical model is a probabilistic graphical model (a type of

statistical model) that represents a set of random variables and their conditional dependencies via a directed acyclic graph (DAG). For example, a Bayesian network could represent the probabilistic relationships between diseases and symptoms. Given symptoms, the network can be used to compute the probabilities of the presence of various diseases.

Words and Phrases

unwittingly /ʌnˈwɪtɪŋlɪ/ *adv.*
   unintentionally 无意地

node /nəʊd/ *n.*
   point at which a curve crosses itself 节点

whereabouts /ˈhweərəbaʊts/ *n.*
   place where sb. is 某人所在的地方

pinpoint /ˈpɪnpɔɪnt/ *v.*
   to discover or show exactly where it is 准确定位

advocate /ˈædvəkeɪt/ *n.*
   person who supports or speaks in favor of a cause, policy, etc. 拥护者

recoil /ˈrɪkɔɪl/ *v.*
   to draw oneself back in fear 畏缩;退缩

infectious /ɪnˈfekʃəs/ *adj.*
   (of a disease) caused by bacteria, etc. that are passed on from one person to another 传染的

authentication /ɔːˌθentɪˈkeɪʃn/ *n.*
   proving (sth.) to be valid or genuine or true 证实

spouse /spaʊs/ *n.*
   husband or wife 配偶

overlap /ˌəʊvəˈlæp/ *v.*
   partly cover (sth.) by extending over its edge 部分重叠

indiscrete /ˌɪndɪˈskriːt/ *adj.*

not divisible or divided into parts 不分开的；一体的

glitch /glɪtʃ/ *n.*

problem that stop sth. from working properly 故障

anonymous /əˈnɒnɪməs/ *adj.*

written or given by sb. who does not reveal his name 匿名的

butler /ˈbʌtlə(r)/ *n.*

chief male servant of a house 男管家

Reading Comprehension Questions

1. The main idea of the passage is _____ .

    (A) it's wrong for us to leak important information online

    (B) the danger of leaking your personal information on line may be greater than you think

    (C) the friends we make via Tweets and Facebook are unreliable

    (D) the systems Tweets and Facebook have developed can identify people who might spread infectious diseases

2. Which message does not fit the author's descriptions about the dynamic Bayesian network? _____

    (A) Its predicting accuracy can be improved by any existing information about the person's whereabouts.

    (B) Even person who has never shared their location can be located with 47 percent accuracy.

    (C) It could help contact friends nearby to prevent suicide attempts.

    (D) It protects you against strangers rather than friends.

3. By saying "You can imagine looping this process over and over" in paragraph 6 Sadilek means that _____ .

    (A) users will protect their privacy in horror

    (B) this work will be presented at the Web Search and Data Mining conference in Seattle

(C) the nodes in the target person's network determines the target's most likely location

(D) the model is likely to make predictions about every Twitter user

4. Which message fits the description of the social authentication system rolled out by Facebook? _____

(A) It can effectively block those suspicious logins.

(B) It protects you against both strangers and friends.

(C) It can help one protect against strangers by removing intimate friends.

(D) It was designed to block suspicious logins but it had some flaws.

5. In which way does the new programming language called Jeeves help to solve the problem of online privacy leaking? _____

(A) It enforces privacy policies automatically.

(B) It substitute the value of variables with the software depending on who the user is.

(C) It lets a programmer delegate privacy responsibilities and concentrate on the actual function of their code.

(D) All the above.

(选文、注释:马仁蓉)

3. The End of the Full-Time Salaried Job

By Dan Schawbel[1]

1   In 1997, author Dan Pink noted in an article in *Fast Company*[2] magazine that there were approximately 25 million "free agents" in the U.S.. A free agent, much like in sports, is a person who does not have any commitments that restrict their actions, and it includes all non-salaried jobs. Free agents are also referred to as contract workers, consultants and freelancers. They don't receive health care benefits, unemployment insurance or collective bargaining[3] rights. Free agents work with multiple clients on a variety of projects based on their unique set of abilities.

2   In 2011, Kelly Services[4] found that the number of free agents had grown to 44 million as Americans desired more freedom, flexibility and ways to get paid for their professional skills. Recently, a study by MBO Partners[5] projected that there could be 70 million free agents by 2020, creating a workplace environment with more free agents than full-time employees. That shows that we're moving from an economy that supported full-time employment and benefits to one where professionals have multiple jobs simultaneously.

3   Companies are hiring more free agents than ever before because they save money and acquire niche expertise to solve specific business problems. This is different from full-time salaried workers who get benefits and are generalists in their fields. In 2009, companies hired 28 percent more freelancers, and now in 2012, they are hiring 36 percent more, reports CareerBuilder John Challenger, the CEO of Challenger, Gray & Christmas, says that "another benefit of hiring freelancers is that during slow periods, [companies] don't have to hold onto them". Companies are moving toward a "hire at will" recruiting strategy and away from a "hire for life" one.

4 ① In the current economy, there is no job security, it's easy for professionals to become irrelevant with the explosion of new technology, and employees are building their careers across organizations, not just up the ladder. The social contract that employers have with workers is evolving to one where "it's less about loyalty and more important to focus on projects", says Challenger. So if you're a free agent, or aspiring to be one, here are a few important tips to keep in mind.

(1) **Bond Together with Other Free Agents**

5 ② The biggest challenge you will have is to build a pipeline of client projects to survive and thrive on. There can be periods of time when you're looking for the next project, unlike a full-time gig where your manager delivers the next project right to you. You have to be a good salesperson and be able to develop relationships if you want to last in the business. One way around this is to connect with other like-minded free agents and become "master tradesmen", as Challenger says. This way, you will have more control over contracting out your expertise. By bonding together, you can share resources and have ongoing interactions with clients in a more scalable manner. You should refer jobs to other free agents because they might reciprocate in the future. The karma you create by helping out other people will pay dividends later. Use Twellow.com to search for freelance professionals on Twitter and join the Consultants Group on LinkedIn of more than 200,000 people to start connecting with other free agents today.

(2) **Tap into Freelance Marketplaces**

6 ③ Don't bother searching on Google for freelance gigs because you might be competing with foreign companies who can do work cheaper than you. Gigs that pay well and are in high demand include online marketing, writing specialized material for businesses and media outlets, computer programming and copywriting. Gigs that don't pay well are blogging, new business development and graphic design. There are websites where you can bid on new projects, blogs with their own job boards and aggregation sites that compile

opportunities for you. For starters, you can review thousands of open projects on Elance.com and bid on the appropriate ones that match your skill set. Next, you can submit your résumé to job boards on niche blogs, like jobs.problogger.net, for blogging gigs. Finally, you can use aggregation sites like Indeed.com to explore thousands of freelance jobs by keyword. By signing up for these services, it will force you to stay connected to freelance-job postings. As a bonus, you can use Twitter Search to review new opportunities in real time.

(3) **Sell Yourself Constantly**

7   Whenever you're not working on a client project, you should be getting your name out there. This may become a full-time job when you start your freelance career, but as you grow your client base, it will turn into a part-time job, consuming about 15 hours out of your week. Create a website that shows case studies, your bio, a client list and samples of your work. From there, you should be going to industry events, blogging about your business, speaking at local associations and conferences, creating an e-mail newsletter to keep clients and potentials engaged, and writing articles for trade magazines and websites. ④ You should also ask your satisfied clients for referrals and, if you have the funds, you should advertise your services using Google AdWords, Facebook Social Ads and LinkedIn. You want as many people to know about you as possible because they will be the word-of-mouth engine that builds your business.

(4) **Turn Your Projects into a Full-Time Position**

8   One third of all freelancers are looking for full-time work, says the Bureau of Labor Statistics. Some free agents may prefer a full-time salaried job with benefits. While you're working with clients, search their job boards and ask your contacts about open positions when you see them. ⑤ Start to look at your client as your employer by working longer hours, proposing solutions to problems and attending company events. Let your client know that you want to work for them full-time, because if they don't know you're interested, they won't think about you when a position opens. Although you may be working

harder for the same amount of money, you will be in the best position to capitalize on a full-time position. By putting the effort in, you're showing them that you're committed, loyal and deserving of the position.

(From *The Washington Post*, January 5, 2012.)

Notes

[1] **Dan Schawbel**: Managing Partner of Millennial Branding, a Gen Y research and consulting firm, Dan Schawbel is the author of the No. 1 international bestselling book, *Me 2.0: 4 Steps to Building Your Future*, now in 13 languages. His second book is called *Promote Yourself: The New Rules For Career Success*. Dan is a columnist at both *TIME* and *FORBES*, and has been featured in over 1,000 media outlets, such as "The Today Show" on *NBC*, "Street Signs" on *CNBC*, "The Nightly Business Report" on *PBS*, "The Willis Report" on *Fox Business*.

[2] **Fast Company**: A full-color business magazine, *Fast Company* releases 10 issues per year and focuses on technology, business, and design. Robert Safian has been the editor-in-chief since 2007, having previously worked at *Fortune*, *Time*, and *Money*. The magazine has won numerous industry awards.

[3] **Collective Bargaining**: A process of negotiation between employers and a group of employees, collective bargaining aims at reaching agreements to regulate working conditions. The interests of the employees are commonly presented by representatives of a trade union to which the employees belong. The collective agreements reached by these negotiations usually set out wage scales, working hours, training, health and safety, overtime, grievance mechanisms, and rights to participate in workplace or company affairs.

[4] **Kelly Services**: An American temporary staffing agency that operates throughout the world. It is headquartered in Troy, Michigan, and offers services that include temporary staffing services, outsourcing, vendor on-site

and full-time placement. Kelly operates in 41 countries and territories. Kelly employs more than 530,000 individuals annually, in areas including office services, accounting, engineering, information technology, law, science, marketing, creative services, light industrial, education, and health care.

[5] **MBO Partners**: A business services company based in Herndon, VA, U.S.A.. MBO Partners offers a business operating platform designed to support the solo-practitioner or a multi-person consulting practice. MBO Partners also offers its consultant customers access to business insurance, workers compensation, payroll administration, tax payments, health benefits, life insurance, and disability insurance.

Words and Phrases

commitment /kəˈmɪtmənt/ *n.*

a promise to do something or to behave in a particular way 承诺；许诺

niche /nɪtʃ/ *n.*

(business) an opportunity to sell a particular product to a particular group of people 有利可图的缺口；商机

generalist /ˈdʒenrəlɪst/ *n.*

a person who has knowledge of several different subjects or activities 通才；多面手

pipeline /ˈpaɪplaɪn/ *n.*

a series of pipes that are usually underground and are used for carrying oil, gas, etc. over long distances 输油管道；渠道

gig /gɪg/ *n.*

(North American English, informal) a job, especially a temporary one 临时工作

ongoing /ˈɒngəʊɪŋ/ *adj.*

continuing to exist or develop 进行的；前进的

scalable /ˈskeɪləbl/ *adj.*

designed to work on a large or small scale, according to needs 可升级的

reciprocate /rɪˈsɪprəkeɪt/ *v.*

to behave or feel towards somebody in the same way as they behave or feel towards you 回报;互换

karma /ˈkɑːmə/ *n.*

good/ bad karma (informal) the good/ bad effect of doing a particular thing, being in a particular place, etc. 因果报应;因缘

dividend /ˈdɪvɪdend/ *n.*

an amount of the profits that a company pays to people who own shares in the company 分红;红利

outlet /ˈaʊtlet/ *n.*

a way of expressing or making good use of strong feelings, ideas or energy 出口;发泄通道

blog /blɒg/ *v.*

to keep a blog; to write something in a blog 博客

aggregation /ˌægrɪˈgeɪʃn/ *n.*

the act of putting together different items, amounts, etc. into a single group or total 聚集;集合

compile /kəmˈpaɪl/ *v.*

to produce a book, list, report, etc. by bringing together different items, articles, songs, etc. 编制;汇编

bonus /ˈbəʊnəs/ *n.*

(usually singular) anything pleasant that is extra and more or better than you were expecting 奖金;额外津贴

bio /ˈbaɪəʊ/ *n.*

(in nouns, adjectives and adverbs) connected with living things or human life: biodegradable; biography 个人简介

newsletter /ˈnjuːzletə(r)/ *n.*

a printed report containing news of the activities of a club or organization that is sent regularly to all its members 时事通讯

capitalize /ˈkæpɪtəlaɪz/ v.

(business) to sell possessions in order to change them into money   积累资本；使……资本化

hold onto

to keep something for somebody else or for longer than usual   紧紧抓住

contract out

choose to withdraw from or not become involved in a scheme   拒绝参加

capitalize on/upon sth.

to gain a further advantage for yourself from a situation   从某事物中获利；投机倒把

Suggested Topics for Writing

1. Nowadays, some people prefer to work in a big enterprise while others prefer to stay in a small business or start their own business. What do you prefer to do in face of the job market? Write an essay on this issue and give specific evidence to support your idea.

2. American writer Leonard R. Sayles once said: "We are not conscious of the extent to which work provides the psychological satisfaction that can make the difference between a full and an empty life." Do you agree or disagree with this statement? Write an essay to give your comment on his idea.

(选文:徐守平;注释:丁菲菲)

Unit Two Individual Growth

1. The Essence of Charm

By Laurie Lee[1]

1   Charm is the ultimate weapon, the supreme seduction, against which there are few defenses. If you've got it, you need neither money, looks, nor pedigree. It's a gift, given only to give away, and the more used, the more there is. It is also a climate of behavior set for perpetual summer and thermostatically controlled by taste and tact.

2   True charm is an aura, an invisible musk in the air; if you see it working, the spell is broken. Charm is dynamic, and cannot be turned on and off at will. As to its ingredients, there is no fixed formula. A whole range of mysteries goes into the caldron, but the magic it offers must be absolute — one cannot be "almost" or "partly" charmed.

3   ① In a woman, charm is probably more exacting than in a man, requiring a wider array of subtleties. It is a light in the face, an air of exclusive welcome, an almost impossibly sustained note of satisfaction in one's company, and regret without fuss at parting. A woman with charm finds no man dull; indeed, in her presence he becomes not just a different person but the person he most wants to be. Such a woman gives life to his deep-held fantasies by adding the necessary conviction to his long suspicion that he is the king.

4   Of those women who have most successfully charmed me I remember

chiefly their voices and eyes. Their voices were intimate and enveloping. The listening eyes, supreme charm in a woman, betrayed no concern with any other world than this, warmly wrapping one round with total attention and turning one's lightest words to gold. Theirs was a charm that must have continued to exist, like the flower in the desert, even when there was nobody there to see it.

5   ② <u>A woman's charm spreads round her that particular glow of well-being for which any man will want to seek her out and, by making full use of her nature, celebrates the fact of his maleness and so gives him an extra shot of life. Her charm lies also in that air of timeless maternalism, that calm and pacifying presence, which can dispel a man's moments of frustration and anger and restore his failures of will.</u>

6   Charm in a man, I suppose, is his ability to capture the complicity of a woman by a single-minded acknowledgment of her uniqueness. Here again it is a question of being totally absorbed, of really forgetting that anyone else exists, for nothing more fatally betrays than the suggestion of a wandering eye. Silent devotion is fine, but seldom sufficient; ③ <u>it is what a man says that counts, the bold declarations, the flights of fancy, the uncovering of secret virtues.</u> A man is charmed through his eyes, a woman by what she hears, so no man need to be too anxious about his age. As wizened Voltaire[2] once said: "Give me a few minutes to talk away my face and I can seduce the Queen of France."

7   But charm isn't exclusively sexual; it comes in a variety of cooler flavors. Most children have it — till they are told they have it — and so do old people with nothing to lose; animals, too, of course. With children and smaller animals, it is often in the shape of the head and in the chaste unaccusing stare; with young girls and ponies, a certain stumbling awkwardness, a leggy inability to control their bodies. But all these are passive and appeal by capturing one's protective instincts.

8   You know who has charm. But can you acquire it? Properly, you can't, because it's an originality of touch you have to be born with. Or it's something

that grows naturally out of another quality, like the simple desire to make people happy. ④ Certainly, charm is not a question of learning palpable tricks, like wrinkling your nose, or having a laugh in your voice. On the other hand, there is an antenna, a built-in awareness of others, which most people have, and which care can nourish.

9   But in a study of charm, what else does one look for? Apart from the ability to listen — rarest of all human virtues — apart from warmth, sensitivity, and the power to please, there is a generosity which makes no demands. Charm spends itself willingly on young and old alike, on the poor, the ugly, the dim, the boring, on the last fat man in the corner. It reveals itself also in a sense of ease, in casual but perfect manners, and often in a physical grace which springs less from an accident of youth than from a confident serenity of mind. Any person with this is more than just a popular fellow; he is also a social healer.

10   Charm, in the end, is a most potent act of behavior, the laying down of a carpet by one person for another to give his existence a moment of honor. ⑤ It is close to love in that it moves without force, bearing gifts like the growth of daylight. It snares completely, but is never punitive. It disarms by being itself disarmed, strikes without wounds, wins wars without casualties — though not, of course, without victims.

11   In the armory of man, charm is the enchanted dart, light and subtle as a hummingbird. But it is deceptive in one thing — like a sense of humor, if you think you've got it, you probably haven't.

(From *Essays for Explication*, CBS Publishing, 1984)

Notes

[1] **Laurie Lee**: Born on June 26, 1914, Slad, near Stroud, Gloucestershire, England, died on May 13, 1997, Slad, English poet and prose writer, best known for *Cider with Rosie* (1959), a memoir of the author's

boyhood in the Cotswold countryside. Educated in his home village and in nearby Stroud, Lee eventually moved to London and traveled in Spain in the mid-1930s. Upon his return to England, he worked as a film-script writer (1940 – 1943) and as an editor for *the Ministry of Information* (1944 – 1945). Lee published several volumes of poetry in the 1940s and 1950s, but he achieved little recognition until his autobiographical book *Cider with Rosie*.

[2] **Voltaire**: Pseudonym of Francois-Marie Arouet, was born on November 21, 1694, Paris, died on May 30, 1778, Paris, one of the greatest of all French writers. Although only a few of his works are still read, he continues to be held in worldwide repute as a courageous crusader against tyranny, bigotry and cruelty. Through its critical capacity, wit and satire, Voltaire's work vigorously propagates an ideal of progress to which people of all nations have remained responsive.

Words and Phrases

pedigree /'pedɪgriː/ *n.*
 a person's family history or the background of something, especially when this is impressive   门第；世系

perpetual /pə'petjuəl/ *adj.*
 (of a job or position) lasting for the whole of somebody's life   终身的；永久的

aura /'ɔːrə/ *n.*
 (of sth.) a feeling or particular quality that is very noticeable and seems to surround a person or place   气氛

subtlety /'sʌtltɪ/ *n.*
 the small but important details or aspects of something   精妙之处

maternalism /mə'tɜːnəlɪzəm/ *n.*
 the quality of having or showing the tenderness and warmth and affection of or befitting a mother   母性

pacify /ˈpæsɪfaɪ/ v.

to make somebody who is angry or upset become calm and quiet 抚慰

dispel /dɪsˈpel/ v.

to make something, especially a feeling or belief, go away or disappear 消除；驱散

wizened /ˈwɪzənd/ adj.

looking smaller and having many folds and lines in the skin, because of being old 多皱的；因年老而干瘪的

chaste /tʃeɪst/ adj.

simple and plain in style; not decorated 纯朴的；未修饰的

stumble /ˈstʌmbl/ v.

to make mistakes, or hesitate in reading, speaking or playing music 不顺畅地说、读或演奏

pony /ˈpəʊnɪ/ n.

a type of small horse 小型马；矮马

palpable /ˈpælpəbl/ adj.

that is easily noticed by the mind or the senses 明显的；易察觉的

antenna /ænˈtenə/ n.

either of the two long thin parts on the heads of some insects and some animals that live in shells, used to feel and touch things with 触角

generosity /ˌdʒenəˈrɒsətɪ/ n.

(to/towards sb.) the fact of being generous (= willing to give somebody money, gifts, time or kindness freely) 慷慨

potent /ˈpəʊtənt/ adj.

having a strong effect on your body or mind; powerful 有强效的；强有力的

snare /sneə/ v.

to catch something, especially an animal, in a snare 设陷阱捕捉

punitive /ˈpjuːnɪtɪv/ adj.

very severe and that people find very difficult to pay 苛刻的

casualty /ˈkæʒuəlti/ *n.*

a person that suffers or a thing that is destroyed when something else takes place 伤亡

armory /ˈɑːməri/ *n.*

a place where arms are kept 军械库

enchanted /ɪnˈtʃɑːntɪd/ *adj.*

put (someone or something) under a spell 中魔法的；着魔的

dart /dɑːt/ *n.*

a small pointed object, sometimes with feathers to help it fly, that is shot as a weapon or thrown in the game of darts 飞镖

deceptive /dɪˈseptɪv/ *adj.*

likely to make you believe that something is not true 欺骗性的

set for

(usually passive) to keep something for a special use or purpose 为……而准备；布置；分配

at will

whenever or wherever you like 任意；随意

seek out

(seek sb. out) to look for and find somebody, especially when this means using a lot of effort 挑选出

lie in (sth.)

(of ideas, qualities, problems, etc.) to exist or be found 存在；在于

apart from

in addition to; as well as 除了……外还；此外

lay (sth.) down

to put something down, especially on the floor, ready to be used 铺；铺放

Reading Comprehension Questions

1. According to paragraph 3, a charming woman finds no man dull, because _____.

    (A) as long as she is present, he becomes a different person

    (B) she receives any man with lightened face and exclusive welcome

    (C) her charm wakes his desire to be a powerfully charming person

    (D) she never suppress her satisfaction in a man's company

2. The word "exacting" in paragraph 3 probably means _____.

    (A) demanding   (B) precise

    (C) detailed   (D) careful

3. The author quotes Voltaire in the end of paragraph 6 to suggest that _____.

    (A) a man will successfully capture a woman's heart by his charming voice

    (B) a man's silent devotion is not enough to successfully seduce a woman

    (C) a charming man holds the belief that every woman is as unique as a Queen

    (D) a woman cares more about what a man says rather than how he looks

4. It can be inferred from paragraph 7 that _____.

    (A) children and old people are charming in a similar way to men and women

    (B) children's charm is spontaneous and they don't know they have it until they are told

    (C) people's protective instincts signify children and animals' charm

    (D) old people is charming because they have nothing to lose

5. From paragraph 8, we can figure out that charm _____.

    (A) can not be acquired by us, because it is a quality that needs original efforts

    (B) can be acquired by us, because it can grow out of another quality

(C) can not be acquired by us, because it is not as easy as learning palpable tricks

(D) can be acquired by those who pay enough attention to other peoples' feelings

(选文、注释:何朝阳)

2. Average Is Over

By Thomas L. Friedman[1]

1　A big mismatch exists today between how U.S. CEO's look at the world and how many American politicians and parents look at the world — and it may be preventing us from taking our education challenge as seriously as we must.

2　① For many politicians, "outsourcing" is a four-letter word because it involves jobs leaving "here" and going "there". But for many CEO's, outsourcing is over. In today's seamlessly connected world, there is no "out" and no "in" anymore. There is only the "good", "better" and "best" places to get work done, and if they don't tap into the best, most cost-efficient venue wherever that is, their competition will.

3　For politicians, it's all about "made in America", but, for CEO's, it is increasingly about "made in the world" — a world where more and more products are now imagined everywhere, designed everywhere, manufactured everywhere in global supply chains and sold everywhere. American politicians are still citizens of our states and cities, while CEO's are increasingly citizens of the world, with mixed loyalties. For politicians, all their customers are here; for CEO's, 90 percent of their new customers are abroad. The credo of the politician today is: "Why are you not hiring more people here?" The credo of the CEO today is: "You only hire someone — anywhere — if you absolutely have to," if a smarter machine, robot or computer program is not available.

4　Yes, this is a simplification, but the trend is accurate. The trend is that for more and more jobs, average is over. ② Thanks to the merger of, and advances in, globalization and the information technology revolution, every boss now has cheaper, easier access to more above-average software, automation, robotics, cheap labor and cheap genius than ever before. So just doing a job in an average way will not return an average lifestyle any longer. Yes, I know, that's what they said about the Japanese "threat" in the 1980s. But Japan, alas, challenged just two American industries — cars and consumer electronics — and just one American town, Detroit. Globalization and the Internet/telecom/computing revolution together challenge every town, worker and job. There is no good job today that does not require more and better education to get it, hold it or advance in it.

5   Which is why it is disturbing when more studies show that American K-12 schools continue to lag behind other major industrialized countries on the international education tests. Like politicians, too many parents think if their kid's school is doing better than the one next door, they're fine.

6   ③ Well, a dose of reality is on the way thanks to Andreas Schleicher and his team at the Organization for Economic Cooperation and Development[2], which coordinates the Program for International Student Assessment, known as the PISA test. Every three years, the OECD has been giving the PISA test to a sample of 15-year-olds, now in 70 countries, to evaluate reading, math and science skills. The U.S. does not stand out. It's just average, but many parents are sure their kids are above average. With help from several foundations in the U.S., Schleicher has just finished a pilot study of 100 American schools to enable principals, teachers and parents to see how their own schools stack up against similar schools in the best-educated countries, like Finland and Singapore.

7   ④ "The entry ticket to the middle class today is a postsecondary education of some kind, but too many kids are not coming out of K-12 prepared for that, and too many parents don't get it," says Jon Schnur, the chairman of America Achieves, which is partnering with the OECD. on this project as part of an effort to help every American understand the connection between educational attainment at their school — for all age groups — and what will be required to perform the jobs of the future.

8 "Imagine, in a few years, you could sign onto a Website and see this is how my school compares with a similar school anywhere in the world," says Schleicher. "And then you take this information to your local superintendent and ask: 'Why are we not doing as well as schools in China or Finland?' "

9 Schleicher's team is assessing all their test results — and socioeconomic profiles of each school — to make sure they have a proper data set for making global comparisons. They hope to have the comparison platform available early next year.

10 Says Schleicher: "If parents do not know, they will not demand, as consumers, a high quality of educational service. They will just say the school my kids are going to is as good as the school I went to." If this comparison platform can be built at this micro scale, he says, it could "lead to empowerment at the really decisive level" of parents, principals and teachers demanding something better.

11 ⑤ "This is not about threatening schools," he adds. It is about giving each of them "the levers to effect change" and a window into the pace of change that is possible when every stakeholder in a school has the data and can say: Look at those who have made dramatic improvements around the world. Why can't we?

(Form *The New York Times*, August 7, 2012)

Notes

[1] **Thomas L. Friedman**: Born on July 20, 1953, is an American journalist, columnist and author. He has won the Pulitzer Prize three times and currently writes a weekly column for *The New York Times*. He has written extensively on foreign affairs, global trade, globalization, and environmental issues.

[2] **The Organization for Economic Co-operation and Development (OECD)**: An influential research and policy-making body that sets international standards

on a wide range of issues including communications technologies and the future of the Internet. The OECD is comprised of 34 member countries, which include mostly developed nations, but also emerging states such as Mexico, Chile and Turkey. It provides a forum for comparative policy discussions between governments that seek answers to common problems, identify best practices and encourage coordination between domestic and international policies.

Words and Phrases

mismatch /ˈmɪsmætʃ/ *n.*
 a combination of things or people that do not go together well or are not suitable for each other　不协调

outsource /ˈaʊtsɔːs/ *v.*
 to arrange for sb. outside a company to do work or provide goods for the company　外包

cost-efficient /ˈkɒstɪˈfɪʃnt/ *adj.*
 cost-effective　有成本效益的

venue /ˈvenjuː/ *n.*
 a place where people meet for an organized event, for example a concert, sporting event or conference　会场

credo /ˈkriːdəʊ/ *n.*
 a set of beliefs, principles, or opinions that strongly influence the way a person lives or works　信条

K-12 /ˈkeɪtuːˈtwelv/ *adj.*
 (in the U.S.) relating to education from kindergarten to 12th grade　从幼儿园到12年级教育的

superintendent /ˌsuːpərɪnˈtendənt/ *n.*
 a person who has a lot of authority and manages and controls an activity, a place, a group of workers, etc.　主管

profile /ˈprəʊfaɪl/ *n.*

a description of sb./sth. that gives useful information 简况;轮廓

empowerment /ɪmˈpaʊəmənt/ *n.*

the process of giving a person or a group of people power and status in a particular situation 赋权

stack up against to be as good as sb./sth. else 比得上

Reading Comprehension Questions

1. What may be the result of the "mismatch" mentioned in paragraph 1? _____
   (A) Job creation in America
   (B) The increase of new consumers
   (C) The manufacture of more products
   (D) A negative effect on American education

2. The word "outsourcing" (line 1, paragraph 2) most probably means _____.
   (A) going abroad
   (B) contracting work out
   (C) connecting the world
   (D) seeking jobs in other countries

3. The way U.S. CEO's look at the world is the product of _____.
   (A) fierce competition
   (B) their credo and mixed loyalties
   (C) the Japanese "threat" in the 1980s
   (D) globalization and the information technology revolution

4. Which of the following is true according the text? _____
   (A) Every good job requires better education to hold it.
   (B) American secondary schools continue to stand out.
   (C) More and more American CEO's come from other countries.

(D) College graduates cannot afford the entry ticket to the middle class.

5. Many parents are sure that their children are above average because _____ .

(A) they are unable to make global comparisons

(B) American schools are among the best in the world

(C) Schleicher's pilot study does not involve all American schools

(D) they do not demand a high quality of educational service

(选文、注释:任爱军)

3. Are You a Striver, Slacker or Fantasist?

By Simon Kuper[1]

In truth, real people are usually a mix of the three archetypes, but most people tend towards one particular type.

1 It may be the defining London sight: people walking up escalators at Tube[2] stations. In this city only tourists stand goggling blankly into space. That's because London — like Manhattan, and other great cities — has fallen into the hands of strivers. They are driving everyone else out of town.

2 Philosophers and pop psychologists spent centuries trying to explain humankind, but only in 1996 did the South African novelist Jo-Anne Richards[3] and I finally identify the three basic human types: strivers, slackers and fantasists.

3 ① Strivers are restless overachievers who walk up escalators. Their habitats include the City of London and Davos. Almost all political leaders are strivers, except ones who inherited their position, such as George W. Bush. As Richards explains in a now-dead book proposal: "Strivers start companies, build skyscrapers and finish marathons. But not all strivers rule the world. They also make the trains run on time, and organise charities." A working-class female striver might become a head nurse. If the job market sidelines women altogether, she will strive vicariously, through her children. "Strivers," writes Richards, "have the energy and discipline to make other people's dreams come true." Strivers make every minute count, and devote their leisure-time to self-improvement. Their drugs of choice are accelerators: coffee and cocaine.

4 By contrast, slackers do nothing. "They prefer to avoid effort rather than

pursue pleasure," writes Richards. "This in itself can be exhausting." ② It's hard to name any well-known slackers, because by definition slackers rarely become famous, except by accident. Sometimes a slacker will get an idea for a novel or for creating world peace, but then she sinks back into the sofa and the moment passes. Whereas business newspapers celebrate strivers, slacker newspapers celebrate lottery winners. Andrew Lamprecht, in his seminal article on slackers, writes that although they have "no idea what they want from life" they often compensate with "a catholic knowledge of television".

5 If slackers devote their leisure time to anything, it's extended adolescent hobbies such as surfing or collecting comics. Their drugs of choice are anaesthetics: vodka or cigarettes.

6 ③ The third human type, the fantasist, lives inside his imagination. Fantasists have little desire to impose themselves on the world. A fantasist might spend years writing a short story, then discard it. Fantasists are never efficient and always miss deadlines. They are suckers for new age fads such as crystals. They do create a lot of art, which strivers buy. Fantasist drugs of choice stimulate fantasy: marijuana or ecstasy. When people are presented with the three human archetypes, most claim to be fantasists.

7 ④ In truth, real people are usually a mix of the three archetypes. For instance, successful artists such as Steven Spielberg or Damien Hirst are generally striver-fantasists. However, most people tend towards one particular type: for instance, someone might be slacker-dominant, with fantasist streaks.

8 Naturally the three types irritate each other. A fantasist friend once told me an idea he had for a book. Being a striver, I began to strategize about finding a publisher. The more I talked, the less enthusiastic my friend became. Eventually, he changed the subject. He never intended to write the book. He just liked imagining it.

9 We strivers are even more at odds with slackers. Our force fields clash with theirs: our very presence makes them stressed, as if we were human deadlines. You see this clash in politics, where striver rulers are always

exhorting slacker populations to pull their socks up: in Nicolas Sarkozy[4]'s formulation: "Work harder to earn more." Rulers hate the notion that someone somewhere might be slacking. Soviet leaders were forever promoting bricklaying contests or rationing vodka, unaware that they were fighting human nature. But slackers rarely revolt against striver rule. Instead, they dream up conspiracy theories.

10 No wonder the three archetypes have tended to segregate themselves. In big cities, strivers gravitate to financial districts, whereas fantasists establish enclaves such as Greenwich Village[5] in 1950s New York or Belleville in today's Paris. When strivers discover these enclaves and drive up prices, fantasists create more distant enclaves. Slackers generally avoid big cities, often preferring the parental home, writes Richards.

11 ⑤ In the U.S., with its great geographic mobility, the separation of the three types was always marked. Strivers headed for Manhattan and Washington, whereas slackers preferred places such as Miami. You sense each city's dominant mode the minute you arrive: at JFK airport in New York, the lady running the cab rank bellows, "Move it along, people! You, sir, take this cab." She's on her way up. At Miami airport, you can't even find cabs.

12 However, segregation of the three human types is now proceeding faster than ever before. Rising house prices and growing inequality are driving non-strivers out of big cities, and even out of previously fantasist coastal towns such as Cape Town[6] and San Francisco. Slackers and fantasists must be upset, but unless you read blogs their voices go unheard, and they certainly won't do anything about it.

(From *Financial Times*, February 3, 2012)

Notes

[1] **Simon Kuper** (1969 –): Born in Uganda and grew up in London, the Netherlands, the U.S., Sweden and Jamaica, he studied at Oxford, Harvard and the Technical University of West Berlin. He now lives with his family in Paris. His first book, *Football Against the Enemy* (1994), set him on a path of writing about the world with an anthropologist's eye.

[2] **The Tube**: The underground railway system in London.

[3] **Jo-Anne Richards**: A South African journalist and an internationally published novelist with a PhD in Creative Writing from Wits University.

[4] **Nicolas Sarkozy** (1955 –): A French politician who served as the President of France and Co-Prince of Andorra from May 16 2007 until May 15 2012.

[5] **Greenwich Village**: A district of New York City on the lower west side of Manhattan, traditionally associated with writers, artists, and musicians.

[6] **Cape Town**: The legislative capital of South Africa and administrative capital of the province of Western Cape.

Words and Phrases

striver /ˈstraɪvə/ n.

a person who makes great efforts to achieve or obtain something 拼搏者

slacker /ˈslækə(r)/ n.

a person who avoids work or effort 游手好闲者

fantasist /ˈfæntəsɪst/ n.

a person who imagines or dreams about something 幻想者

archetype /ˈɑːkiˌtaɪp/ n.

a very typical example of a certain person or thing 原型

goggle /ˈɡɒɡl/ v.

look with wide open eyes, typically in amazement 凝视

habitat /ˈhæbɪtæt/ n.

the natural home or environment of an animal, plant, or other organism 栖息地

sideline /ˈsaɪdlaɪn/ v.

remove from the centre of activity or attention; place in a less influential position 使退出

anaesthetic /ˌænəsˈθetɪk/ n.

a substance that induces insensitivity to pain 麻醉剂

ecstasy /ˈekstəsi/ n.

an overwhelming feeling of great happiness or joyful excitement 狂喜

exhort /ɪgˈzɔːt/ v.

strongly encourage or urge (someone) to do something 劝告

segregate /ˈsegrɪˌgeɪt/ v.

set apart from the rest or from each other; isolate or divide 隔离

gravitate /ˈgrævɪteɪt/ v.

move towards or be attracted to a person or thing 被吸引

at odds

in conflict 争执;不一致

Suggested Topics for Writing

1. "When people succeed, it is because of hard work. Luck has nothing to do with success." Do you agree or disagree with the quotation above? Use specific reasons and examples to explain your position.

2. Some people are always in a hurry to go places and get things done. Other people prefer to take their time and live life at a slower pace. Which do you prefer? Use specific reasons and examples to support your answer.

(选文、注释:斯骏)

Unit Three   Youth Today

1. How Those Spoiled Millennials Will Make the Workplace Better for Everyone

By Emily Matchar[1]

1　Have you heard the one about the kid who got his mom to call his boss and ask for a raise? Or about the college student who quit her summer internship because it forbade Facebook in the office?

2　① Yep, we're talking about Generation Y — loosely defined as those born between 1982 and 1999 — also known as millennials. Perhaps you know them by their other media-generated nicknames: teacup kids, for their supposed emotional fragility; boomerang kids, who always wind up back home; trophy kids — everyone's a winner; the Peter Pan[2] generation, who'll never grow up.

3　Now this pampered, over-praised, relentlessly self-confident generation is flooding the workplace. They'll make up 75 percent of the American workforce by 2025 — and they're trying to change everything.

4　These are the kids, after all, who text their dads from meetings. They think "business casual" includes skinny jeans. And they expect the company president to listen to their "brilliant ideas".

5　When will they adapt?

6   ② They won't. Ever. Instead, through their sense of entitlement and inflated self-esteem, they'll make the modern workplace adapt to them. And we should thank them for it. Because the modern workplace frankly stinks, and the changes wrought by Gen Y will be good for everybody.

7   The current corporate culture simply doesn't make sense to much of middle-class Gen Y. Since the cradle, these privileged kids have been offered autonomy, control and choices. They've been encouraged to show their creativity and to take their extracurricular interests seriously. Raised by parents who wanted to be friends with their kids, they're used to seeing their elders as peers rather than authority figures. When they want something, they're not afraid to say so.

8   And what the college-educated Gen Y-ers entering the workforce want is engaging, meaningful, flexible work that doesn't take over their lives. ③ The grim economy and lack of job opportunities don't seem to be adjusting their expectations downward much, either. According to a recent AP[3] analysis, more than 53 percent of recent college grads are unemployed or underemployed, but such numbers don't appear to keep these new grads from thinking their job owes them something.

9   According to surveys, 50 percent of Gen Y-ers would rather be unemployed than stay in a job they hate. Unlike their child- and mortgage-saddled elders, many can afford to be choosy about their jobs, given their notorious reliance on their parents. After all, they can always move back in with Mom and Dad, who are likely to be giving them financial help well into their 20s.

10   In fact, it's possible that a bad economy can make being choosy even easier — if more people are struggling to find work and living at home, there's no stigma to it.

11   ④ Despite the recession, or perhaps because of it, corporations are eager to hire and retain the best, most talented Gen Y workers. "In this risky economic environment, the energy, insight and high-tech know-how of Gen

Y-ers will be essential for all high-performing organizations," said a 2009 study on Gen Y from Deloitte, the professional services giant.

12　Companies are beginning to heed Gen Y's demands. Though flextime and job-sharing have been staples of the workforce for a few decades, they are becoming more accepted, even in rigid corporate culture, says Laura Schildkraut, a career counselor specializing in the needs of Gen Y. There has also been a rise in new work policies, such as ROWE, or "results only work environment", a system in which employees are evaluated on their productivity, not the hours they keep. In a ROWE office, the whole team can take off for a 4 p.m. "Spider-Man" showing if they've gotten enough done that day.

13　Radical-sounding perks such as unlimited paid vacation — assuming you've finished your pressing projects — are more common among companies concerned with attracting and retaining young talent. By 2010, 1 percent of U.S. companies had adopted this previously unheard-of policy, largely in response to the demands of Generation Y.

14　The Deloitte study warns that, to retain Gen Y-ers, companies "must foster a culture of respect that extends to all employees, regardless of age or level in the organization". In other words, Treat your Gen Y workers nicely. But we should be treating everyone nicely already, shouldn't we?

15　Beyond that, Gen Y's demands may eventually help bring about the family-friendly policies for which working mothers have been leading the fight. Though *the Family and Medical Leave Act of 1993* afforded some protections for working parents, genuine flexibility is still a privilege of the lucky few, and parents who try to leave the office at 5:30 p.m. are often accused of not pulling their weight. Well, guess what? Now everybody wants to leave the office at 5:30 p.m. Because they've got band practice. Or dinner with their grandma. Or they need to walk their rescue puppy.

16　The American workplace has been transformed during upswings and downturns. The weekend was a product of labor union demands during the relative boom of the early 20th century. The Great Depression[4] led to *the New*

Deal's Fair Labor Standards Act, which introduced the 40-hour workweek and overtime pay to most Americans. But now, workplace change is coming from unadulterated, unorganized worker pushiness.

17 ⑤ So we could continue to roll our eyes at Gen Y, accuse them of being spoiled and entitled and clueless little brats. We could wish that they'd get taken down a peg by the "school of hard knocks" and learn to accept that this is just the way things are.

18 But if we're smart, we'll cheer them on. Be selfish, Gen Y! Be entitled! Demand what you want. Because we want it, too.

(From *The Washington Post*, August 16, 2012)

Notes

[1] **Emily Matchar** (1982–): Born in North Carolina, the United States, graduated from Harvard University in 2004. Her work has appeared in *The Atlantic*, *Salon*, *The Washington Post*, *Time*, *The New Republic*, *Gourmet*, and *Outside*, among others. She has made numerous appearances on TV and radio, including *The Colbert Report*, *Good Morning America*, *MSNBC's The Cycle*, *NPR*, and *BBC*.

[2] **Peter Pan**: Referring to a person who looks unusually young for their age, or who behaves in a way that would be more appropriate for somebody younger. Originated from a story by J. M. Barrie about a boy with magic powers who never grew up.

[3] **AP**: Associated Press, cooperative news agency, the oldest and the largest in the U. S. and the largest in the world. More than 15,000 organizations worldwide obtain news, photographs, and illustrations from the agency.

[4] **Great Depression**: Depression of 1929, the longest and most severe economic depression ever experienced by the Western world. It began in the

U.S. with the New York Stock Market Crash of 1929 and lasted until about 1939. Since the U.S. was the major creditor and financier of postwar Europe, the U.S. financial collapse led to collapses of other economies, especially those of Germany and Britain. The Great Depression contributed to political upheaval. It led to the election of Franklin Roosevelt in the U.S. and major changes in the structure of the U.S. economy brought about by his New Deal. It directly contributed to Adolf Hitler's rise to power in Germany in 1933 and to political extremism in other countries.

Words and Phrases

entitlement /ɪnˈtaɪtlmənt/ *n.*

the official right to have or do sth. 权利，资格

stink /stɪŋk/ *v.*

to seem very bad, unpleasant, or dishonest 让人觉得很糟糕；令人厌恶

stigma /ˈstɪgmə/ *n.*

feelings of disapproval that people have about particular illnesses or ways of behaving 耻辱

heed /hiːd/ *v.*

to pay careful attention to sb.'s advice or warning; take notice of 听从

staple /ˈsteɪpl/ *n.*

a large important part of sth. 主要部分；重要内容

perk /pɜːk/ *n.*

something you receive as well as your wages for doing a particular job 补贴，额外待遇

upswing /ˈʌpswɪŋ/ *n.*

a situation in which sth. improves or increases over a period of time 改进；上升

pull one's weight

to work as hard as everyone else in a job, an activity, etc. 尽本分；尽职责

take sb. down a peg

to make sb. realize that they are not as good, important, etc. as they think they are 挫某人的锐气

school of hard knocks

the (sometimes painful) education one gets from life's usually negative experiences that makes sb. less confident or successful, often contrasted with formal education 把人锤炼成才的逆境,"社会大学"

Reading Comprehension Questions

1. The author suggests that Gen Y's sense of entitlement and inflated self-esteem comes mainly from _____.

    (A) their upbringing

    (B) their school education

    (C) the modern workplace

    (D) the current corporate culture

2. The author thinks that millennials _____.

    (A) are too demanding

    (B) will never mature

    (C) are emotionally fragile

    (D) will make the workplace better for everyone

3. According to the author, what keeps Gen Y-ers from having to lower their expectations of work? _____.

    (A) Financial help from the government

    (B) Their reliance on their parents

    (C) Their self-esteem

    (D) Their creativity

4. The demands of Generation Y have resulted in _____.

    (A) new work policies

(B) higher unemployment

(C) the introduction of flextime

(D) high-performing organizations

5. The author uses the phrase "unadulterated, unorganized worker pushiness" (the last three paragraph) to describe _____.

(A) labor unions

(B) Gen Y workers

(C) working mothers

(D) the whole workforce

(选文:任爱军;注释:许振宇)

2. Harvard Cheating Scandal:
Is Academic Dishonesty on the Rise?

By Erika Christakis[1] and Nicholas A. Christakis[2]

In order to better understand what leads students to cheat, colleges and universities need to break the code of silence and apply their own academic methods to the problem.

1   Harvard University's announcement last week of an investigation into a case of widespread cheating offered a little thrill of schadenfreude for some: confirmation, perhaps, that a venerable 376-year-old institution — whose motto, "Veritas", means truth in Latin — could be caught up in the same pedestrian crimes and misdemeanors found at less lofty altitudes. According to reports in the *Harvard Crimson*[3], more than 100 students in an undergraduate lecture class are alleged to have lifted material from shared study guides on a final take-home exam.

2   ① Moral indignation is an understandable response, and can have a role in all sorts of problems. But focusing on individual character flaws or moral failings obscures both the magnitude and the complexity of the problem of our national crisis of academic dishonesty. Cheating cuts to the very heart of academia, more so than it does other institutions that have faced similar wrongdoing, such as professional sports and the financial industry, because the search for truth is the primary mission of a university. Harvard's public statement promised appropriate discipline for the wrongdoers and noted that the "vast majority" of its students do their own work. Such circumstances — which are dismayingly common on college and high school campuses nationwide — often prompt institutions to reassert community values in this way. But a

broader kind of soul searching is required.

3 Students have cheated for as long as there have been schools, but by any measure, academic dishonesty is on the rise. While detection methods and increased vigilance explain some of this increase, most experts believe the incidence of the forms of cheating has increased too. ② <u>For one thing, the technological ease of mashup culture can make it hard for students to recognize — or care — that they are appropriating the work of others. In fact, according to reporting in *the New York Times*, some of the Harvard students involved seemed to think that they didn't really cheat, that there were special circumstances in the class, that the professor changed the rules and so on.</u>

4 Our experience at Harvard College as house masters of one of the 12 undergraduate residential-academic communities gives us a bird's-eye view of the pressures that can drive students to temptation. We've observed two types of students who are especially vulnerable.

5 ③ <u>The first type is prone to panic and self-doubt. Feeling the weight of family or societal expectations, these students become so worried about failure that they lose perspective and fail to see obvious alternatives to cheating like asking for help before things get out of control, making up a failed class over the summer, taking time off, being honest with their parents or learning to cope with a plan B.</u> Because of their youth and immaturity, these students don't realize that bombing a class isn't a permanent blot on their record as a human being and will not likely affect their long-term capacity to find a job or get into graduate school. The tunnel vision of late adolescence, which can be so energizing in other arenas, takes on a toxicity that inhibits resilience in the face of disappointment.

6 The second type of student at risk for cheating belongs to one or more social networks like fraternities, "final clubs", athletic teams or cultural-affinity groups, where barriers to cheating (like social opprobrium) are lower and the logistic means to cheat (like sharing study materials) is more common. ④ <u>Membership in these networks often comes with a high degree of loyalty and</u>

social pressure to perpetuate cheating or protect cheaters from discovery. In fact, there is evidence that peer attitudes to cheating help predict who will engage in academic dishonesty.

7   But on some level, everyone is at risk for academic dishonesty, no matter who or where they are. Nowadays, we seem to live in a culture of lies. Should we really be surprised that high schoolers cheat on standardized tests when they grow up among adults — Olympic cyclists, politicians, money managers, high school administrators, journalists, professors and even their own parents — who may be thrifty, at best, with the truth? It doesn't help to whisk away such a widespread phenomenon by dividing the world into good and bad people or insisting that the whole business is simply beyond our control.

8   ⑤ The right response to cheating involves not just adjudicating the individual cases but also exploring and addressing the structural determinants and risk factors for academic dishonesty. For guidance, academic institutions can look within their own community. Many scholars are already at the vanguard of understanding how decent people fall prey to the pressures of groupthink and poor decisionmaking. For example, Dan Ariely, a behavioral economist at Duke University, describes some of the science behind the contagion of cheating norms in his recent book, *The (Honest) Truth About Dishonesty*. We need to learn more about the learning environments that either promote or inhibit academic integrity.

9   As with any epidemiological study that addresses risk factors, people may not like the results. But we should embrace, not fear, these kinds of findings. They may shine light on dysfunctional social and academic practices that are in need of change, but educators and students nationwide need to engage in this difficult self-reflection. It will be a real test of Veritas.

(From *Time*, September 4, 2012)

Notes

[1] **Erika Christakis**: An early childhood educator at the Yale Child Study Center.

[2] **Nicholas A. Christakis**: The co-director of the Institute of Network Science at Yale University, is an American sociologist and physician known for his research on social networks and on the socioeconomic and biosocial determinants of behavior, health, and longevity. Nicholas was named to the *TIME 100* in 2009.

[3] *Harvard Crimson*: The daily student newspaper of Harvard University founded in 1873. It is the only daily newspaper in Cambridge, Massachusetts, and is run entirely by Harvard College undergraduates.

Words and Phrases

Schadenfreude /ˈʃɑːdnfrɔɪdə/ n.

(from German) a feeling of pleasure at the bad things that happen to other people 幸灾乐祸

magnitude /ˈmæɡnɪtjuːd/ n.

the great importance of sth. 重大;重要性

reassert /ˌriːəˈsɜːt/ v.

to make other people recognize again your tight or authority to do sth., after a period when this has been in doubt 重申;坚持

vigilance /ˈvɪdʒɪləns/ n.

state or quality of being very careful to notice any signs of danger or trouble; watchfulness 警惕;警惕性

mashup /ˈmæʃʌp/ n.

a combination of elements from different sources used to create a new song, video, computer file, program, etc. 混搭,跨界

resilience /rɪˈzɪliəns/ *n.*

the ability of people or things to feel better quickly after sth. unpleasant, such as shock, injury, etc. 快速恢复的能力；适应力

opprobrium /əˈprəʊbriəm/ *n.*

severe criticism of a person, country, etc. by a large group of people 谴责，抨击

perpetuate /pəˈpetʃueɪt/ *v.*

to make sth. such as a bad situation, a belief, etc. continue for a long time 使持续；使永久化

adjudicate /əˈdʒuːdɪkeɪt/ *v.*

to make an official decision about who is right in a disagreement between two groups or organizations 裁决，判决

vanguard /ˈvæŋɡɑːd/ *n.*

the leaders of a movement in society, for example, in politics, art, industry, etc. 领导者，先驱

contagion /kənˈteɪdʒən/ *n.*

sth. bad that spreads quickly by being passed from person to person 传播，扩散

epidemiological /ˌepɪˌdiːmɪəˈlɒdʒɪkl/ *adj.*

of the scientific study of the spread and control of diseases 流行病学的

dysfunctional /dɪsˈfʌŋkʃənl/ *adj.*

not working normally or properly 机能失调的；功能障碍的

be prone to

be likely to suffer from sth. or to do sth. bad 易于遭受

fall prey to

(of a person) to be harmed or affected by sth. bad 受害；受坏的影响

Suggested Topics for Writing

1. Some people say that nowadays we seem to live in a culture of lies and therefore we can turn a blind eye to school cheating. Other people think differently. What's your idea about this issue? Please give specific evidence to support your idea.

2. An old saying goes: "Honesty is the best policy." Please make a comment on this old saying.

(选文:徐守平;注释:许振宇)

Unit Four Social Concerns

1. The Price of Marriage in China

By Brook Larmer[1]

1 ① From the entrance of an H & M store in Joy City, a Beijing shopping mall, Yang Jing seemed lost in thought, tapping her nails on her iPhone 4S. But her eyes kept moving. They tracked the clusters of young women zigzagging from Zara to Calvin Klein Jeans. They lingered on a face, a gesture, and then moved on, searching. "This is a good place to hunt," she told me. "I always have good luck here."

2 Ms. Yang, 28, is one of China's premier love hunters, a new breed of matchmaker that has proliferated in the country's economic boom. The company she works for, Diamond Love and Marriage, caters to China's nouveaux riches: men, and occasionally women, willing to pay tens and even hundreds of thousands of dollars to outsource the search for their ideal spouse.

3 In Joy City, Ms. Yang gave instructions to her eight-scout team, one of six squads the company was deploying in three cities for one Shanghai millionaire. This client had provided a list of requirements for his future wife, including her age (22 to 26), skin color ("white as porcelain") and sexual history (yes, a virgin).

4 ② Three miles away, in a Beijing park near the Temple of Heaven, a woman named Yu Jia jostled for space under a grove of elms. A widowed 67-

year-old pensioner, she was clearing a spot on the ground for a sign she had scrawled for her son. "Seeking Marriage," read the wrinkled sheet of paper, which Ms. Yu held in place with a few fragments of brick and stone. "Male. Single. Born in 1972. Height 172 cm. High school education. Job in Beijing."

5 Ms. Yu is another kind of love hunter: a parent seeking a spouse for an adult child in the so-called marriage markets that have popped up in parks across the city. Long rows of graying men and women sat in front of signs listing their children's qualifications.

6 Ms. Yu's crude sign had no flourishes: no photograph, no blood type, no zodiac sign, no line about income or assets. Unlike the millionaire's wish list, the sign didn't even specify what sort of wife her son wanted. "We don't have much choice," she explained. "At this point, we can't rule anybody out."

7 In the four years she has been seeking a wife for her son, Zhao Yong, there have been only a handful of prospects. Even so, when a woman in a green plastic visor paused to scan her sign that day, Ms. Yu put on a bright smile and told of her son's fine character and good looks. The woman asked: "Does he own an apartment in Beijing?" Ms. Yu's smile wilted, and the woman moved on.

8 As recently as 1990, researchers found that a vast majority of residents in two of China's largest cities dated just one person before marriage: their prospective spouse.

9 ③ China's transition to a market economy has swept away many restrictions in people's lives. This may be a time of sexual and romantic liberation in China, but the solemn task of finding a husband or wife is proving to be a vexing proposition for rich and poor alike.

10 "The old family and social networks that people used to rely on for finding a husband or wife have fallen apart," said James Farrer, an American sociologist. "There's a sense of dislocation in China, and some young people don't know where to turn."

11 The confusion surrounding marriage in China reflects a country in

transition. Inequalities of wealth have created new fault lines[2] in society, while the largest rural-to-urban migration in history has blurred many of the old ones. As many as 300 million rural Chinese have moved to cities in the last three decades. Uprooted and without nearby relatives to help arrange meetings with potential partners, these migrants are likely to be lost in the swell of the big city.

12　Demographic changes, too, are creating complications. Not only are many more Chinese women postponing marriage to pursue careers, but China's gender gap — 118 boys are born for every 100 girls. By the end of this decade, researchers estimate, the country will have a surplus of 24 million unmarried men.

13　④ China's matchmaking tradition stretches back more than 2,000 years, to the first imperial marriage broker in the late Zhou dynasty. The goal of matchmakers ever since has usually been to pair families of equal stature for the greater social good. Today, however, matchmaking has warped into a commercial free-for-all in which marriage is viewed as an opportunity to leap up the social ladder or to proclaim one's arrival at the top by someone.

14　Single men have a hard time making the list if they don't own a house or an apartment, which in cities like Beijing are extremely expensive. And despite the gender imbalance, Chinese women face intense pressure to be married before the age of 28, lest they be rejected and stigmatized as "leftover women[3]".

15　Over the last year, I tracked the progress of two matchmaking efforts at the opposite extremes of wealth. Together, they help illuminate the forces reshaping marriage in China.

16　⑤ In one case, Ms. Yu's migrant son reluctantly agreed to allow his aging mother to make the search for his future wife her all-consuming mission. In the other, Ms. Yang's richest client at Diamond Love deployed dozens of love hunters to find the most exquisite fair-skinned beauty in the land, even as he fretted about being conned by a baijinnü, or gold digger.

17　Between the two extremes is Ms. Yang herself, whose very success as a love hunter has made her the breadwinner in her own family. Despite her growing discomfort with the sexism that permeates the love-hunting business, she has sympathy for her superrich clients.

18　"They worked hard, made a lot of money, and left their old world behind. Now they don't have time to find a wife, and they don't know whom to trust. So they come to us." She said.

(From *The New York Times*, March 9, 2013)

Notes

[1] **Brook Larmer**: Independent writing and editing professional and the author of *Operation Yao Ming*.

[2] **Fault Lines**: Lines dividing a society into different camps, which is likely to cause problems.

[3] **Leftover Women**: "Shengnü", a derogatory term that classifies women who remain unmarried in their late twenties and beyond. Similarly, "shengnan" or "leftover men" has also been used.

Words and Phrases

cluster /ˈklʌstə(r)/ n.

　a group of people, animals or things close together　群

premier /ˈpremɪə(r)/ adj.

　most important, famous, or successful　最成功的

proliferate /prəˈlɪfəreɪt/ v.

　to increase rapidly in number or amount　猛增

outsource /ˈaʊtsɔːrs/ v.

　to arrange for sb. outside a company to do work or provide goods for that company 外包

spouse /spaʊs/ *n.*

a husband or wife 配偶

squad /skwɒd/ *n.*

a group of people who have a particular task 小组

deploy /dɪˈplɔɪ/ *v.*

to move soldiers or weapons into a position where they are ready for military action 部署

porcelain /ˈpɔːsəlɪn/ *n.*

a hard white shiny substance made by baking clay and used for making delicate cups, plates and decorative objects 瓷

jostle /ˈdʒɒsl/ *v.*

to push roughly against sb. in a crowd 挤

grove /grəʊv/ *n.*

a small group of trees 小树林

elm /elm/ *n.*

a tall tree with broad leaves 榆树

scrawl /skrɔl/ *v.*

to write sth. in a careless untidy way, making it difficult to read 潦草地写

visor /ˈvaɪzə(r)/ *n.*

a curved piece of plastic, etc. worn on the head above the eyes to protect them from the sun 遮阳帽舌

wilt /wɪlt/ *v.*

to become weak or tired or less confident 发蔫

vex /veks/ *v.*

to annoy or trouble sb. 使烦恼

proposition /ˌprɒpəˈzɪʃn/ *n.*

a thing that you intend to do; a problem or task to be dealt with 任务

sociologist /ˌsəʊsiˈɒlədʒɪst/ *n.*

one who study sociology 社会学家

dislocate /ˈdɪsləkeɪt/ v.

to stop a system, plan, etc. from working or continuing in the normal way 使混乱

migration /maɪˈgreɪʃn/ n.

the movement of large number of people, birds or animals from one place to another 移居

blur /blɜː(r)/ v.

to become or make sth. become difficult to distinguish clearly 难以区分

demographic /ˌdeməˈgræfɪk/ adj.

related to the population and different groups within it 人口的

stature /ˈstætʃə(r)/ n.

the importance and respect that a person has because of their ability and achievements 声望，名望

warp /wɔːp/ v.

(sth.) make sth. become twisted 扭曲

proclaim /prəˈkleɪm/ v.

to show sth. clearly, to be a sign of sth. 表明

stigmatize /ˈstɪgmətaɪz/ v.

to treat sb. in a way that makes them feel that they are very bad or unimportant 侮蔑

illuminate /ɪˈluːmɪneɪt/ v.

to make sth. clearer or easier to understand 解释

migrant /ˈmaɪgrənt/ n.

a person who moves from one place to another, especially in order to find work 移民

exquisite /ɪkˈskwɪzɪt/ adj.

extremely beautiful or carefully made 精美的

con /kɒn/ v.

to trick sb. especially in order to get money from them or persuade them to do sth. for you 欺骗

permeate /ˈpɜːmieɪt/ v.

(of an idea, an influence, a feeling, etc.) to affect every part of sth. 感染，传播

nouveaux rich

a person who has recently become rich and likes to show how rich they are in a very obvious way 暴发户

linger on

to continue to look at sb./sth. or think about sth. for longer than usual 持续看

cater to

to provide the things that a particular type of person wants, especially things that you'd on approve of 满足需要

the zodiac signs

the twelve imaginary areas in the sky in which the sun, moon, and planets appear to lie, each with a special name and symbol 黄道十二宫

marriage broker

a person who is paid to arrange for two people to meet and marry 媒人

fret about

to be worried or unhappy and not able to relax 苦恼

Reading Comprehension Questions

1. Why was Yang Jing standing at the entrance of a Beijing shopping mall? _____

    (A) To find potential wife for a rich man.

    (B) To wait for a potential buyer for her iPhone 4S.

    (C) To meet one important friend.

    (D) To try her luck in a bargain.

2. What problem did Yu Jia have in finding a spouse for her son? _____

(A) Her sign was crude with no flourishes.

(B) Her son didn't own an apartment in Beijing.

(C) She was picky in choosing a daughter-in-law.

(D) She couldn't provide any qualifications concerning her son.

3. James Farrer thinks there is a sense of dislocation in China because _____.

(A) as many as 300 million rural Chinese have moved to cities in the last three decades

(B) a vast majority of residents in China dated just one person before marriage

(C) finding a husband or wife is proving to be a vexing proposition for rich and poor alike

(D) many people are without the help they used to have

4. By saying "Single men have a hard time making the list", the author means that single men _____.

(A) find it difficult to find a spouse

(B) feel it hard to choose a wife from a list

(C) have trouble putting themselves into a list

(D) encounter obstacles to get in touch with girls

5. Why does Ms. Yang have a growing discomfort? _____

(A) Her client wants her to find the most exquisite fair-skinned beauty in the land.

(B) She is being conned by a gold digger.

(C) She encounters prejudice in her job.

(D) She has sympathy for her superrich clients.

(选文:徐守平;注释:陈静)

2. Will There Be Any Nature Left?

By Michael Marshall[1]

1   On the face of it, the future of the natural world looks grim. Humans are causing a mass extinction that will be among the worst in Earth's history. Wilderness is being razed and we are filling the air, water and land with pollution.

2   ① <u>The bottom line is that, barring a radical shift in human behavior, our distant descendants will live in a world severely depleted of nature's wonders.</u>

3   ② <u>Biodiversity, in particular, will be hit hard. Assessments of the state of affairs make consistently depressing reading. Almost a fifth of vertebrates are classed as threatened, meaning there is a significant chance that those species will die out within 50 years.</u>

4   The main cause is habitat destruction, but human-made climate change will be increasingly important. One much-discussed model estimates that between 15 and 37 percent of species will be "committed to extinction" by 2050 as a result of warming.

5   "It will be a new world", says Kate Jones at the Institute of Zoology in London, U.K.. The ecosystem will become much simpler, dominated by a small number of widespread, populous species. "Among animals that are 'incompatible' with humans — we may like hunting them or colonizing their habitat, for example — few will survive. I don't have much hope for blue macaws, pandas, rhinos or tigers," Jones says.

6   Ultimately, though, life will recover: it always has. ③ <u>The mass extinctions of the past offer hints as to how the ecosystem will eventually bounce back</u>, says Mike Benton at the University of Bristol, U.K.. The two that we know most about are the end-Permian extinction[2] 252 million years

ago, which wiped out 80 percent of species, and the less severe end-Cretaceous extinction[3] 65 million years ago, which famously took out the dinosaurs. The Permian extinction is more relevant because it was caused by massive global warming, but Benton cautions that the world was very different then, so today's mass extinction will not play out in quite the same way.

7   Recoveries usually have two stages. If ours pans out in the same way, the first 2 to 3 million years will be dominated by fast-reproducing, short-lived "disaster taxa". These will rapidly give rise to new species and bring the world's species count back up.

8   But a lot of things will be simple, with similar species doing similar things. Herbivores will be less diverse, and top predators may be absent altogether in many places.

9   That's where longer-lived, slower-evolving species come in to restore the full complexity of the ecosystem. But this can take up to 10 million years, much longer than even the most optimistic projections of the human future.

10   It doesn't have to be like that. We can take action now to get the recovery going, although we don't know how much we can accelerate it.

11   ④ Conservation biologists are increasingly thinking the unthinkable, such as relocating species to places where they can thrive while abandoning them to their fate in their native ranges.

12   That may seem unnatural, but given that human influence has already touched almost every ecosystem on Earth, is "natural" even a useful concept any more?

13   ⑤ Even more radically, we might be better off encouraging the formation of new species and ecosystems rather than struggling to save existing species that have no long-term future, like pandas. "There's no way I'd want to get rid of them," says Jones, "but things do change and adapt and die."

14   Benton says the most important thing is to rebuild biodiversity hotspots such as rainforests and coral reefs. That needn't be a gargantuan task. A recent analysis suggests that damaged wetlands can be restored within two human

generations.

15   Beyond that it may be possible to start "evolutionary engineering". For instance we could divide a species into two separate habitats and leave them to evolve separately, or introduce "founder" species into newly rebuilt ecosystems.

16   Nature may solve the problem for us by providing founder species from an unexpected source. Animals such as pigeons, rats and foxes are already flourishing alongside humans and may well give rise to new species, becoming the founders of the new ecosystem.

17   If you are disturbed by the prospect of a world colonized by armies of rapidly evolving rats and pigeons, look away now.

(From *New Scientist*, February 29, 2012)

Notes

[1] **Michael Marshall** (1983–): A British skeptical activist, freelance journalist, public speaker, podcaster, author and blogger. He is co-founder and vice-president of the Merseyside Skeptics Society.

[2] **The End-Permian Extinction**: Colloquially known as the Great Dying or the Great Permian Extinction occurred about 252 Ma (million years) ago, forming the boundary between the Permian and Triassic geologic periods, as well as the Paleozoic and Mesozoic eras. It is the Earth's most severe known extinction event, with up to 96% of all marine species and 70% of terrestrial vertebrate species becoming extinct. It is the only known mass extinction of insects. Some 57% of all families and 83% of all genera became extinct. Because so much biodiversity was lost, the recovery of life on Earth took significantly longer than after any other extinction event, possibly up to 10 million years.

[3] **The End-Cretaceous Extinction**: Refers to the Cretaceous-Paleogene (K-Pg) extinction event, also known as the Cretaceous-Tertiary (K-T)

extinction, was a mass extinction of some three-quarters of plant and animal species on Earth — including all non-avian dinosaurs — that occurred over a geologically short period of time, 66 million years ago. It marked the end of the Cretaceous period and with it, the entire Mesozoic Era, opening the Cenozoic Era that continues today.

Words and Phrases

grim /grɪm/ *adj.*
　unpleasant, depressing　令人沮丧的

extinction /ɪkˈstɪŋkʃn/ *n.*
　state of being no longer in existence　绝种

raze /reɪz/ *v.*
　to destroy completely　彻底破坏

barring /ˈbɑːrɪŋ/ *prep.*
　if there is/are not　如果没有

descendant /dɪˈsendənt/ *n.*
　person having sb. as an ancestor　后代

deplete /dɪˈpliːt/ *v.*
　reduce greatly the quantity of sth.　消耗

vertebrate /ˈvɜːtɪbrət/ *n.*
　animal, bird, etc. having a backbone　脊椎动物

habitat /ˈhæbɪtæt/ *n.*
　natural environment of an animal or a plant　栖息地；产地

macaw /məˈkɔː/ *n.*
　type of large long-tailed tropical American parrot　金刚鹦鹉

Cretaceous /krɪˈteɪʃəs/ *n.*
　of the geological period when chalk-rocks were formed　白垩纪

Permian /ˈpɜːmiən/ *n.*
　of the geological period between Carboniferous and Triassic periods, which

lasted for 60,000,000 years 二叠纪

herbivore /hɜːbɪvɔː(r)/ *n.*

animal that feeds on plants 食草动物

predator /ˈpredətə(r)/ *n.*

animal that kills and eats other animals 食肉动物

projection /prəˈdʒekʃn/ *n.*

estimate of future situations or trends, etc. based on a study of present ones 预测；推断

gargantuan /ɡɑːˈɡæntʃuən/ *adj.*

enormous; gigantic 巨大的

be incompatible with

not consistent or in logical agreement with sth. 不一致

pan out

(of circumstances) develop 发展

Reading Comprehension Questions

1. It's estimated that more species will be extinct by 2050 on account of _____.

    (A) man's hunting

    (B) man's colonizing their habitat

    (C) global warming

    (D) radical shift in human behavior

2. What does "in the same way" mean in paragraph 7? _____.

    (A) Resembling the natural state of the Permian extinction

    (B) Resembling the natural state of Cretaceous extinction

    (C) In the way Mike Benton describes

    (D) In the way dinosaurs disappeared

3. _____ IS NOT the possible way for species recovery.

(A) Encouraging the formation of new species

(B) Relocating species to new places where they can thrive

(C) Saving existing species with no long-term future

(D) Rebuilding hotspots like rainforests and coral reefs

4. Which of the following DOES NOT belong to evolutionary engineering? _____.

(A) Dividing a species into two separate habitats

(B) Leaving the divided species in different habitats to evolve separately

(C) Introducing founder species into newly rebuilt ecosystems

(D) Restoring the damaged wetlands within two human generations

5. The last paragraph implies _____.

(A) the world is colonized by armies

(B) the prospect of the world is disturbing

(C) human beings need to change their behavior

(D) rats and pigeons are already flourishing alongside human

(选文、注释:马仁蓉)

3. A World Without Books?

By Miguel Syjuco[1]

To imagine a world without books is to imagine a world without thought.

1   The novelist Colm Toibin once recounted a story about observing a Cantonese man sitting on a Kowloon[2] footpath reading a book. The man's face was stern with concentration, his finger tracing the line being read. At times the man's expression would screw up in frustration at his progress. Finally, the reader looked up at the sky, his face beaming. ① Whether from a sudden joyous facility with the act of reading, or revelation from what was written, or delight at how the story resolved, it doesn't matter. What mattered is he was in possession of something deliciously private — a connection between him and the writer, between the real world and that world inscribed upon the pages.

2   What would the world be like without books? What a depressing and absurd idea. Scenes like that man reading belie the notion that modern advances pose a threat to reading as we know it.

3   There's always talk that the latest technology signals the demise of the book. Decades ago, radio was what would do it. Then came TV. And now the Internet. ② The machines change, but the act has stayed the same. The simplest form of technology prevails — pages printed into a sheaf and bound between covers. There's something reassuring about such simplicity. Especially when it lets us delve into the complexities of life.

4   Literature is the story of ourselves, the record of who we are, where we came from, and where we're going. Non-fiction illuminates the world for us and fiction explains what non-fiction cannot. Through books we first travel. ③ In those

wanderings we become best acquainted with humanity through the characters we come to know more intimately than anyone else — whether we love, loathe, fear, or fawn over them.

5   The narrator in Kahlil Gibran's *The Prophet*[3] helps me comprehend my faults and aspirations. *Holden Caulfield* and *Harry Potter* make me feel less alone. *King Lear*, *Hannibal Lecter* and *Boromir* are cautionary tales for who we could become if we're not careful. Reading is our deepest connection to what makes us human, and part of a larger society.

6   In that, books are a comfort. When I was a boy with thick glasses and braces on my buckteeth, books were my safe haven. ④ Generations have likewise found solace in the written world, safety in feeling less alone amongst the crowds. Aren't we loneliest, after all, when surrounded by others? But books aren't bomb shelters, they're bridges — through their pages we're brought out into society, and one can posit that someone who reads is prepared for the world on a deeper level than someone who doesn't.

7   Though reading a book connects one with humanity, it is also the last truly private act in a world that's become too public. As nourishment for the mind, it's slow food in a world given over to fast food. Blogs, text messages, e-books, and the like bring topicality, portability, instant gratification, much as newspapers and magazines do.

8   However important such forms are, they endure only as long as the stuff they're printed on. The comforts of books: they defy time, break borders, and repudiate mortality.

9   ⑤ And there are the unquantifiable pleasures that books alone offer: The scent, the sound, the tactile sensation of what is a cerebral, silent, disembodied task. The sharing of a volume by lending it to a friend. The adventure of leaving a book to be found by a stranger, who will in turn partake in that private journey before passing it on again. The grandeur of a civilisation evidenced through its libraries.

10   It is important that we work to give every person the opportunity to enjoy

books as shelters, sustenance, and roads forward. Literacy and library programmes are important goals for developed and developing nations alike. To imagine a world without books is to imagine a world without thought. A world without feeling, compassion, history, or voice.

[From *Reader' Digest*, September 24, 2010]

Notes

[1] **Miguel Syjuco** (1976-): A Filipino writer from Manila and the grand prize winner of the 2008 Man Asian Literary Prize for his first novel *Ilustrado*.

[2] **Kowloon**（九龙）: An urban area in Hong Kong.

[3] ***The Prophet***: A collection of 26 prose poetry essays written in English by the Lebanese artist, philosopher and writer Kahlil Gibran, originally published in 1923. It is Gibran's best known work and has been translated into over 40 different languages and has never been out of print.

Words and Phrases

inscribe /ɪnˈskraɪb/ v.

to write or cut words, your name, etc. onto sth.　在……上写、题、刻

demise /dɪˈmaɪz/ n.

the end or failure of an institution, an idea, a company, etc.　终止

delve /delv/ v.

to search for sth. inside a bag, container, etc.　翻找

aspiration /ˌæspəˈreɪʃn/ n.

a strong desire to have or do sth.　抱负；渴望

solace /ˈsɒləs/ n.

a feeling of emotional comfort when you are sad or disappointed　安慰；慰藉

posit /ˈpɒzɪt/ v.

to suggest or accept that sth. is true so that it can be used as the basis for an argument or discussion 假设；认定

topicality /ˌtɒpɪˈkæləti/ *n*.

the quality of being connected with sth. that is happening or of interest at the present time 时事性；热门话题

repudiate /rɪˈpjuːdieɪt/ *v*.

refuse to accept sth. 拒绝；不接受

tactile /ˈtæktaɪl/ *adj*.

connected with the sense of touch 触觉的

cerebral /ˈserəbrəl/ *adj*.

relating to the brain 大脑的

partake /pɑːˈteɪk/ *v*.

to take part in an activity 参加；参与

sustenance /ˈsʌstənəns/ *n*.

the food and drink that people, animals and plants need to live and stay healthy 营养；养料

screw up

to contract the muscles of your eyes or face because you are in pain, etc. （因疼痛等）眯起眼睛，扭曲面部

Suggested Topics for Writing

1. Do you think modern advances pose a threat to reading as we know it? Use specific reasons and examples to support your answer.

2. "To imagine a world without books is to imagine a world without thought." Do you agree or disagree with the quotation above? Use specific reasons and details to explain your position.

(选文：任爱军；注释：许振宇)

Unit Five Business and Market

1. Things Go Better with Quark?

By Chris Reidy

Think about it: Things go better with Quark? A Rose by any other name may smell as sweet but likely wouldn't sell as well.

1   As Reebok International Ltd.[1] found out last week, coming up with a good name for a new product isn't always easy.

2   "The most important piece of marketing is naming," claims Sam Birger, a cofounder of Whatchamacallit Inc., a small naming firm with offices in Cambridge and Mill Valley, Calif. "It's the handshake, the first impression."

3   Reebok made a bad impression with a shoe it called the Incubus. According to the dictionary, an incubus is an evil spirit who has sex with women while they sleep.

4   Embarrassed, the Stoughton-based footwear giant said it plans to implement new guidelines for checking product names.

5   The art of naming a product or a company is increasingly big business—whether it's done within a company's marketing department or whether outside forces are brought in to help. ① Finding an appropriate, non-offensive name, say companies, can have a direct effect on sales, and in some cases can mean success or failure.

6   Because so many different methods are used, it's hard to say how much

U.S. companies spend on naming new products. Some companies sponsor in-house competitions. Others seek help from their ad agencies and design firms. And still others use naming consultants who can charge anywhere from $20,000 to $250,000 for their services.

7 In return for such fees, these consultants often agree to remain anonymous. Just as some politicians don't like it to be known that their principles were shaped by public opinion polls, many corporations don't like to admit that they needed outside help to come up with a new name.

8 Cadillac used a variety of sources to name its new Catera. A search begun in 1993 reviewed more than a thousand options, including Pegasus, Helios and Ascent, Cadillac said. After winnowing the list several times, eight names were submitted to focus group in "three U.S. cities as well as Paris, Dusseldorf[2] and the Far East," Cadillac said.

9 In part, Catera was chosen for its European flavor and also because the name is inoffensive in a variety of languages, and important consideration in a global economy.

10 ② Indeed, names that are perfectly serviceable in English can suffer in translation. Could Duracell[3]'s name be a factor in why its European battery sales have not always met expectations?

11 Duracell sounds suspiciously like a French phrase that means "difficult to defecate" or "hard stool", said Robert Sprung, chairman of Harvard Translations, a Boston-based foreign language consulting firm with revenues of about $3 million.

12 (Duracell disputes Sprung's interpretation.)

13 Elinor Selame, president of a Newton, [*Massachusetts*]-based firm called Brand-equity International, noted that using a name that makes customers uneasy can cost a company millions of dollars.

14 As an example, she cited the Harlem Savings Bank, which bought another bank in the mid-1980s. ③ When Harlem Savings put its name on some of its newly acquired suburban branches, "deposits walked out the door," Selame

recalled.

15   The bank found that the word Harlem evoked negative connotations for many suburbanites, and it hired Selame's firm to find an agreeable new name. Rechristened the Apple Bank for Savings, the bank quickly gained new customers, Selame said, adding that brand equity doesn't simply choose a name; it seeks to integrate a name with a corporate logo and marketing plan.

16   "Verbal and visual should work hand in hand," she said. "You have to consider how a name will look on signs and business cards and how it will be used in advertising."

17   In the case of the Harlem bank, Selame's company showed it's client a color scheme, a lettering typeface and an advertising tagline: "Apple Bank. We're good for you."

18   "If we had just showed them a name — Apple Bank — they probably would have turned us down," she said.

19   Because new products constantly flood the market, it's hard to find clever names that someone else isn't already using.

20   And, as Avon Products Inc. found out earlier this month, using someone else's name can have unfortunate results.

21   A recent Avon catalog made numerous mentions of the word "Maxx", prompting a lawsuit by the TJX Cos. Of Framingham, which operates the T. J. Maxx chain of offprice apparel stores.

22   To avoid lawsuits, naming consultants often turn to made-up words, and searches for made-up words frequently begin with lists of morphemes. A morpheme, according to linguists, is the smallest fragment of language that conveys meaning.

23   Car companies are especially keen on morpheme-derived names.

24   Using morphemes, a San Francisco firm called Namelab Inc. came up with Acura for the line of luxury cars that Honda introduced in the United States several years ago.

25   The morpheme "acu" connotes precision and care in several languages,

said Ira Bachrach, president of Namelab, a company with about $1.5 million in annual revenues.

26　④ According to Bachrach, the made-up word — Acura — helped exorcise the impression that Japanese companies could make only economy cars that did not deserve to be mentioned in the same breath as Mercedes and BMW.

27　Catera is also supposed to suggest a European commitment to luxury and engineering. Focus groups told Cadillac they thought of a "cat or a fast-moving, agile object" when they heard the word Catera.

28　Lawsuits aren't the only reason to prefer made-up names to real words. In the mid-1980s, a company toyed with calling a computer printer "the Shuttle", but when the space shuttle Challenger blew up, the company became afraid customers would associate the name with a disaster, said linguist Sprung.

29　To generate lists of morpheme-based names, some consultants use computers, but not Namelab, which relies on linguists.

30　"We've wasted a couple of hundred thousand bucks trying to come up with software" to help choose names, Bachrach said.

31　"Intellectually, it's a far more arduous process than you might think," Bachrach said of matching a name to a product.

32　"Whether real or made up, names should be 'short, memorable, relevant' and immune to lawsuit," said Whatchamacllit's Birger.

33　It also helps if a name is easy to pronounce in many languages.

34　By Bachrach's lights, the name Coca-Cola represents a perfect marketing haiku. ⑤ Like a Byronic scholar scanning a poem for rhyme and meter, Bachrach noted that Coca-cola is not only short and visually memorable, but it also pleases the ear by being "alliterative, assonant, repetitive and iambic".

35　Most consultants agree that a great name won't sell a bad product, but opinions can vary about the effect of an unfortunate name on the sales of a good product.

36　In Europe, a U.S. company has had success with a desktop publishing tool called Quark Express even though Quark sounds like a German word for cottage cheese, Sprung said.

37 However, in *The Rechoning*, a book about the auto industry, author David Halberstam noted that the habit of giving cars lame names was one of several reasons why Datsun and Toyota had trouble cracking the U.S. market in the early 1960s.

38 Americans were not enamored of cars with names such as Bluebonnett and Cedric. And a car that Datsun planned to market as the Fair Lady seemed destined to do little better.

39 Then, at the last minute, the name was changed to the 240-Z, and a sports car was on its way to becoming a legend.

(From *The Boston Globe*, February 25, 1997)

Notes

[1] **Reebok International Ltd.**: A global athletic footwear and apparel company. Reebok produces and distributes fitness and sports items including shoes, workout clothing and accessories, and training equipment. The company was founded in 1895 as J. W. Foster and Sons in Bolton, Lancashire, England. It was later renamed Reebok and has been operating as a subsidiary of Adidas since 2005. The global headquarters are located in Canton, Massachusetts.

[2] **Dusseldorf**: An industrial city of northwest Germany, on the Rhine, capital of North Rhine-Westphalia.

[3] **Duracell**: An American brand product line of batteries and smart power systems formerly owned by Procter & Gamble. In November 2014, Berkshire Hathaway announced its intent to acquire the brand for 4.7 billion U.S. dollars. The acquisition received regulatory approval from the European Commission in July 2015, and is due to be completed in early 2016.

Words and Phrases

winnow /ˈwɪnəʊ/ v.

remove (people or things) from a group until only the best ones are left 遴选

apparel /əˈpærəl/ *n.*

clothing 服装；衣服

linguist /ˈlɪŋgwɪst/ *n.*

a person who studies languages or linguistics 语言学家

exorcise /ˈeksɔːˌsaɪz/ *vt.*

drive out or attempt to drive out (a supposed evil spirit) from a person or place; completely remove (something unpleasant) from one's mind or memory 驱除

haiku /ˈhaɪkuː/ *n.*

a Japanese poem of seventeen syllables, in three lines of five, seven, and five, traditionally evoking images of the natural world 俳句；三行俳句诗

meter /ˈmiːtə(r)/ *n.*

the rhythm of a piece of poetry, determined by the number and length of feet in a line 诗的格律、韵律

alliterative /əˈlɪtəreɪtɪv/ *adj.*

begin with same consonant 头韵的；用头韵法的

assonant /ˈæsənənt/ *adj.*

two or more similar sounds 类韵的

assonance /ˈæsənəns/ *n.*

resemblance of sound between syllables of nearby words, arising particularly from the rhyming of two or more stressed vowels, but not consonants (e.g., sonnet, porridge), but also from the use of identical consonants with different vowels (e.g., killed, cold, culled) 谐音，类韵

iambic /aɪˈæmbɪk/ *adj.*

using a rhythm in poetry, consisting of one short or unstressed syllable followed by one long or stressed syllable 抑扬格的

Reading Comprehension Questions

1. Which of the following is true according to the first three paragraphs? _____

   (A) Producing a good product is not always easy.

   (B) Naming a new product well is important.

   (C) A good product will surely sell well.

   (D) Reebok made a shoe of poor quality.

2. To name new products, companies use the following methods except _____.

   (A) sponsoring in-house competitions

   (B) seeking help from their ad agencies and design firm

   (C) using naming consultants

   (D) consulting their lawyers

3. The example of Harlem Savings Bank is to reveal that _____.

   (A) using a name uncomfortable to customers can bring a company great losses

   (B) a name perfectly serviceable in English can suffer in translation

   (C) a good name only can quickly gain customers

   (D) naming firms can be completely relied on for good names

4. Which reason is not mentioned when the author talks about why made-up words are used in naming? _____

   (A) It's hard to find clever names not already used.

   (B) Using someone else's name may prompt a lawsuit.

   (C) A real word name may not attract customers.

   (D) Some real word names may arouse negative association.

5. According to the author, which of the following is not a good name? _____

   (A) Catera.   (B) Acura.

   (C) 240-Z.   (D) Quark Express.

(选文、注释：邹红云)

2. What Is a Bank?

By Lee Ann Obringer

According to Britannica[1].com, a bank is:

An institution that deals in money and its substitutes and provides other financial services. Banks accept deposits and make loans and derive a profit from the difference in the interest rates paid and charged, respectively.

1 Banks are critical to our economy. The primary function of banks is to put their account holders' money to use by lending it out to others who can then use it to buy homes, businesses, send kids to college ...

2 When you deposit your money in the bank, your money goes into a big pool of money along with everyone else's, and your account is credited with the amount of your deposit. When you write checks or make withdrawals, that amount is deducted from your account balance. Interest you earn on your balance is also added to your account.

3 ① <u>Banks create money in the economy by making loans. The amount of money that banks can lend is directly affected by the reserve requirement set by the Federal Reserve. The reserve requirement is currently 3 percent to 10 percent of a bank's total deposits. This amount can be held either in cash on hand or in the bank's reserve account with the Fed.</u> To see how this affects the economy, think about it like this. When a bank gets a deposit of $100, assuming a reserve requirement of 10 percent, the bank can then lend out $90. That $90 goes back into the economy, purchasing goods or services, and usually ends up deposited in another bank. That bank can then lend out $81 of that $90 deposit, and that $81 goes into the economy to purchase goods or

services and ultimately is deposited into another bank that proceeds to lend out a percentage of it.

4　In this way, money grows and flows throughout the community in a much greater amount than physically exists. That $100 makes a much larger ripple in the economy than you may realize!

5　② <u>Banking is all about trust. We trust that the bank will have our money for us when we go to get it. We trust that it will honor the checks we write to pay our bills. The thing that's hard to grasp is the fact that while people are putting money into the bank every day, the bank is lending that same money and more to other people every day. Banks consistently extend more credit than they have cash.</u> That's a little scary; but if you go to the bank and demand your money, you'll get it. However, if everyone goes to the bank at the same time and demands their money (a run on the bank), there might be problem.

6　Even though the Federal Reserve[2] Act requires that banks keep a certain percentage of their money in reserve, if everyone came to withdraw their money at the same time, there wouldn't be enough. In the event of a bank failure, your money is protected as long as the bank is insured by the Federal Deposit Insurance Corporation (FDIC)[3]. The key to the success of banking, however, still lies in the confidence that consumers have in the bank's ability to grow and protect their money. Because banks rely so heavily on consumer trust, and trust depends on the perception of integrity, the banking industry is highly regulated by the government.

7　There are several types of banking institutions, and initially they were quite distinct. Commercial banks were originally set up to provide services for businesses. Now, most commercial banks offer accounts to everyone.

8　Savings banks, savings and loans, cooperative banks and credit unions are actually classified as thrift institutions. Each originally concentrated on meeting specific needs of people who were not covered by commercial banks. Savings banks were originally founded in order to provide a place for lower-income workers to save their money. Savings and loan associations and cooperative banks were established during the 1800s to make it possible for factory workers and other lower-income workers to buy homes. ③ Credit unions were usually started by people who shared a common bond, like working at the same company (usually a factory) or living in the same community. The credit union's main function was to provide emergency loans for people who couldn't get loans from traditional lenders. These loans might be for things like medical costs or home repairs.

9 Now, even though there is still a differentiation between banks and thrifts, they offer many of the same services. Commercial banks can offer car loans, thrift institutions can make commercial loans, and credit unions offer mortgages!

10 ④ Banks are just like other businesses. Their product just happens to be money. Other businesses sell widgets or services; banks sell money — in the form of loans, certificates of deposit (CDs) and other financial products. They make money on the interest they charge on loans because that interest is higher than the interest they pay on depositors' accounts.

11 The interest rate a bank charges its borrowers depends on both the number of people who want to borrow and the amount of money the bank has available to lend. As we mentioned in the previous section, the amount available to lend also depends upon the reserve requirement the Federal Reserve Board has set. At the same time, it may also be affected by the funds rate, which is the interest rate that banks charge each other for short-term loans to meet their reserve requirements.

12 Loaning money is also inherently risky. A bank never really knows if it'll get that money back. Therefore, the riskier the loan the higher the interest rate the bank charges. While paying interest may not seem to be a great financial move in some respects, it really is a small price to pay for using someone else's money. Imagine having to save all of the money you needed in order to buy a house. We wouldn't be able to buy houses until we retired!

13 ⑤ Banks also charge fees for services like checking, ATM access and

overdraft protection. Loans have their own set of fees that go along with them. Another source of income for banks is investments and securities.

(From *How Banks Work*. http://money.howstuffworks.com)

Notes

[1] **Britannica**: The Encyclopedia Britannica, is a general knowledge English-language encyclopedia. The Britannica covers 40 million words on half a million topics.

[2] **The Federal Reserve**: Also known as the Federal Reserve System or simply as the Fed — is the central banking system of the United States. The Fed considers the Federal Reserve System "an independent central bank" because its monetary policy decisions do not have to be approved by the President or anyone else in the executive or legislative branches of government, it does not receive funding appropriated by the Congress, and the terms of the members of the Board of Governors span multiple presidential and congressional terms. If the Federal Reserve wants to ease monetary policy, it will increase the amount of reserves through the purchase of financial assets. Conversely, it can tighten monetary policy through the sale of financial assets.

[3] **Federal Deposit Insurance Corporation (FDIC)**: Independent U.S. government corporation created to insure bank deposits against loss in the event of a bank failure and to regulate certain baking practices. All members of the Federal Reserve System are required to insure their deposits with the FDIC, and almost all commercial banks in the U.S. choose to do so.

Words and Phrases

credit /ˈkredɪt/ *v.*

to add money to a bank account 记入贷方

widget /ˈwɪdʒɪt/ *n.*

a device that is very useful for a particular job 小器具；小装置

overdraft /ˈəʊvədrɑːft/ *n.*

a draft in excess of the credit balance 透支；透支额

security /səˈkjʊərətɪ/ *n.*

a formal declaration that documents a fact of relevance to finance and investment; the holder has a right to receive interest or dividends 有价证券

ripple effect

a situation in which one action causes another, which then causes a third, etc. [= domino effect] 连锁反应

in the event of sth.

used to tell people what they should do if sth. happens 万一；倘若

Reading Comprehension Questions

1. The account balance is _____.

    (A) the amount of money one puts in the bank

    (B) the deposit after credit is calculated

    (C) the money remaining in the deposit account

    (D) the interest after withdrawals

2. That $100 makes a much larger ripple in the economy than you may realize because _____.

    (A) that $100 can be used to purchase goods or services

    (B) a bank can lend it to different customers

    (C) the Federal Reserve sets a low reserve requirement

    (D) different banks will have chances to make use of the $100

3. The role of the government in the banking industry is to _____.

(A) prevent people from withdrawing their money from the bank at the same time

(B) make sure that banks won't go bankrupt

(C) strengthen the bank's ability to grow

(D) ensure the honesty of banking industry

4. In the past credit unions couldn't provide services such as _____.

   (A) sharing a common bond

   (B) offering mortgages

   (C) providing emergency loans

   (D) making commercial loans

5. Which of the following best describes the author's attitude toward borrowing money from banks? _____

   (A) Tolerant.   (B) Disapproval.

   (C) Indifferent.   (D) Pessimistic.

(选文:徐守平;注释:管琛)

3. Why We're Spending So Much on Botox, Makeup and Facelifts

By Martha C. White[1]

1 Last year, Americans spent more on products and procedures to make our faces look better. The reason? Well, it may seem counterintuitive, but experts say the lackluster economy is part of the reason for our collective vanity.

2 The American Society of Plastic Surgeons (ASPS) says that while total cosmetic surgeries fell by 2 percent last year, the number of what they call "minimally invasive procedures"[2] rose by 6 percent. The most popular of these were Botox and Dysport (the brand names for botulinum toxin) injections, followed by soft tissue filler injections, chemical peels, laser hair removal, and microdermabrasion.

3 In 2011, the number of both surgeries and minimally invasive procedures rose, although the uptick in more expensive operations was the smaller increase of the two.

4 "Facial rejuvenation procedures, both surgical and minimally-invasive, experienced the most growth in 2012," an ASPS press release states. That includes a record-high 6.1 million botulinum toxin injections to freeze our frown lines and crows' feet. And although the overall number of surgeries fell, the ASPS says demand for facelifts and eyelid surgeries rose 6 percent and 4 percent, respectively.

5 ① The so-called "lipstick effect"[3] is something consumer psychologists trot out as soon as the economy heads south: The theory goes that we cut back on big-ticket spending, but buy ourselves little indulgences as consolation prizes. Instead of buying a new suit, for example, maybe we'll buy that designer's cologne. Instead of a pair of pricey pumps, we'll settle for the

aforementioned lipstick. Or, in this case, we'll get Botox instead of a pricier nose job or tummy tuck[4]. Maybe we can start calling it the "injection effect" instead.

6　② Unsurprisingly, wealthier Americans seem more willing to keep spending in order to look good. A new survey by Unity Marketing, which examines the spending patterns of affluent Americans, found that the rich are becoming more cautious and keeping those platinum cards[5] in their wallets. But President Pam Danzinger says there are a few spending category outliers.

7　For instance, spending on beauty services increased a whopping 26.5 percent last quarter, "one of the top growth categories in the fourth quarter", Danzinger says in a report accompanying the survey. "Luxury consumers spent more on spa/salon beauty services in the fourth quarter, showing they are still willing to invest to keep up appearances."

8　The same trend can be seen at the makeup counter, too. Last year, we spent 10% more on department store brand skincare products, and 7% more on department store makeup, according to market research firm NPD Group. "We have a clientele that's engaged and wants to buy," says Karen Grant, global industry analyst for beauty.

9　③ All this stuff that we use to make ourselves look good supposedly has a byproduct effect of making us feel good, too. "The reason we hear most is, 'I'll continue to buy beauty because it makes me feel better about myself' ... This driver is more pronounced in the prestige category," Grant says. "There's a more emotional reason than purely logical."

10　The willingness to spend at the upper edge of the price spectrum is even more pronounced, Grant says — and it's not just wealthy Americans dropping big bucks on eye creams and eau de toilettes. People are buying these little luxuries whether they can easily afford them or not, she says. "They'll find the means at the expense of other things."

11　"It's very much an investment. In some cases, you're talking about $300 gift sets and things like that," Grant says.

12   There's some indication that for some of us, this spending could be an investment in our careers — or our love lives.

13   In 2011, Daniel S. Hamermesh, a professor of economics at the University of Texas at Austin and author of *Beauty Pays*, wrote an opinion piece for the *New York Times* spelling out just how much your looks matter in the workplace:

14   One study showed that an American worker who was among the bottom one-seventh in looks, as assessed by randomly chosen observers, earned 10 to 15 percent less per year than a similar worker whose looks were assessed in the top one-third — a lifetime difference, in a typical case, of about $230,000.

15   In an older, equally depressing paper, the Federal Reserve Bank of St. Louis cited Hamermesh's research that an unattractive worker's "plainness penalty" is 9 percent, and that there's a 5 percent "beauty premium" that benefits the pretty and handsome at work.

16   ④ In 2010, the Chicago Tribune noted that older workers aren't just relying on their experience to get ahead in the workplace: They're increasingly trying to turn back the clock with procedures like eye lifts, teeth whitening and hair-loss treatments. "While most older job-seekers know the importance of keeping their skills current, some are applying that same advice to their faces," the article stated.

17   Some recent research also suggests that increased beauty spending is an investment in our romantic futures, particularly for women. In a paper published last year, Sarah Hill, assistant professor of social psychology at Texas Christian University, wrote that recessions make women work harder to try to attract men, and prompt a surge in spending on beauty and cosmetic products and services.

18   ⑤ The basic idea is that recessions create a scarcity of financially stable men, so women compete more aggressively for a smaller number of successful, well-to-do bachelors. In experiments, Hill found that female subjects conditioned to think about a bad economy were more likely to display a

preference for buying items that could enhance their physical appearance.

19   "Consumers may prioritize beauty during times of economic turmoil," she wrote.

(From *Time*. February 27, 2013)

Notes

[1] **Martha C. White**: A native of New Jersey and graduate of Princeton University, resides in upstate New York. She writes about consumer credit, debt and retail banking for TIME.com and previously contributed to AOL's WalletPop.com. She has written about business, finance and the economy for outlets of different kinds.

[2] **Minimally Invasive Procedures**: Include laparoscopic surgery, use state-of-the-art technology to reduce the damage to human tissue when performing surgery.

[3] **Lipstick Effect**: It is a theory that states that during periods of recession or economic downturn, consumers will eschew purchases of big-ticket luxury items and seek material solace in smaller indulgences, such as premium lipstick.

[4] **Tummy Tuck**: A cosmetic surgical operation to remove excess fat, skin, and tissue from the abdomen.

[5] **Platinum Card**: It is a charge card issued by American Express. The Platinum Card was billed as super-exclusive and had a $250 annual fee (it is currently $450). It was offered by invitation only to American Express customers with at least 2 years of tenure, significant spending, and excellent payment history; it is now open to applications on request.

Words and Phrases

counterintuitive   /ˌkaʊntənˈtjuːɪtɪv/   *adj.*

opposite to what seems obvious or natural 反常的

lackluster /ˈlæklʌstə(r)/ *adj.*

lacking energy, excitement, enthusiasm, or passion 无趣味的；单调的

plastic /ˈplæstɪk/ *adj.*

relating to medical operations to improve the appearance of a part of someone's body, either to repair an injury or to make the person more attractive 整形；整容

botulinum /ˌbɑtʃəˈlaɪnəm/ *n.*

a bacterium that causes botulism when it is present in food 肉毒杆菌

toxin /ˈtɒksɪn/ *n.*

a poison produced by a living organism 毒素

microdermabrasion /ˌmaɪkrəʊˌdɜːməˈbreɪʒən/ *adj.*

surgical process that removes scars or other imperfections of the skin by scraping the skin's surface with wire brushes or very fine sandpaper 微晶磨削术

uptick /ˈʌptɪk/

a small increase in the level or value of sth. 小幅上升

rejuvenation /rɪˌdʒuːvəˈneɪʃn/ *n.*

becoming young again 恢复青春；返老还童

consolation /ˌkɒnsəˈleɪʃən/ *n.*

comfort to somebody who is distressed or disappointed 安慰

cologne /kəˈləʊn/ *n.*

a scented liquid with a lighter scent than perfume 古龙香水

outlier /ˈaʊtlaɪə/ *n.*

somebody who chooses not to be a part of a group or community 局外人；另类；孤例

whopping /ˈwɒpɪŋ/ *adj.*

very big or great 巨大的

clientele /ˌklaɪənˈtel/ *n.*

the clients or customers of a professional organization or business, considered as a group 客户

prioritize /praɪˈɔrətaɪz/ v.

to treat a particular job or issue as being more important than any others 优先处理

turmoil /ˈtɜːmɔɪl/ n.

a state of great confusion, commotion, or disturbance 混乱；骚动

trot out

bring out and show for inspection and admiration 提出；炫耀

head south

to lessen in size, strength, or amount 下降

settle for

to accept or agree to something that is not ideal or exactly what was wanted 勉强接受

eau de toilettes

perfume that contains a lot of water and does not smell very strong 淡香水

Suggested Topics for Writing

1. Some people are enthusiastic about improving their appearance by means of cosmetic surgery while others despise artificial beauty. What is your idea about people's investment in facial improvement procedures? Please give specific reasons or examples to support your idea.

2. Brad Tuttle, a researcher at UMass-Amherst, U.S.A., once suggested: "Need Work? You might want to 'have a little work done' on Your Face First." Would you accept his advice, especially with a view to the increasingly competitive job market?

（选文：陈馥梅；注释：徐守平）

Unit Six Technology Development

1. Human Gait Could Soon Power Portable Electronics

By Terry Devitt

1 ① If the vision of Tom Krupenkin and J. Ashley Taylor comes to fruition, one day soon your cellphone — or just about any other portable electronic device — could be powered by simply taking a walk.

2 In a paper appearing this week (August 23) in the journal *Nature Communications*[1], Krupenkin and Taylor, both engineering researchers at the University of Wisconsin-Madison, describe a new energy-harvesting technology that promises to dramatically reduce our dependence on batteries and instead capture the energy of human motion to power portable electronics.

3 "Humans, generally speaking, are very powerful energy-producing machines," explains Krupenkin, a UW-Madison[2] professor of mechanical engineering. "While sprinting, a person can produce as much as a kilowatt of power."

4 Grabbing even a small fraction of that energy, Krupenkin points out, is enough to power a host of mobile electronic devices — everything from laptop computers to cell phones to flashlights. "What has been lacking is a mechanical-to-electrical energy conversion technology that would work well for this type of

application," he says.

5   Current energy harvesting technologies are aimed at either high-power applications such as wind or solar power, or very low-power applications such as calculators, watches or sensors. "What's been missing," says Taylor, "is the power in the watts range. That's the power range needed for portable electronics."

6   Solar power, the researchers explain, can also be used to power portable electronics, but, unlike human motion, direct sunlight is usually not a readily available source of energy for mobile electronics users.

7   In their *Nature Communications* report, Krupenkin and Taylor describe a novel energy-harvesting technology known as "reverse electrowetting", a phenomenon discovered by the Wisconsin researchers. The mechanical energy is converted to electrical energy by using a micro-fluidic device consisting of thousands of liquid micro-droplets interacting with a novel nano-structured substrate.

8   This technology could enable a novel footwear-embedded energy harvester that captures energy produced by humans during walking, which is normally lost as heat, and converts it into up to 20 watts of electrical power that can be used to power mobile electronic devices. ② <u>Unlike a traditional battery, the energy harvester never needs to be recharged, as the new energy is constantly generated during the normal walking process.</u>

9   The initial development of this technology was funded by a National Science Foundation Small Business Innovation Research grant. Now Krupenkin and Taylor are seeking to commercialize the technology through a company they've established, InStep NanoPower.

10   ③ <u>In their work, Taylor and Krupenkin were inspired by severe limitations that current battery technology imposes on mobile electronics users.</u> As any cellphone or laptop user knows, heavy reliance on batteries greatly restricts the utility of mobile electronic devices in many situations. What's more, many mobile electronics are used in remote areas of the world where

electrical grids for recharging batteries are often not available. Cellphone users in developing countries often have to pay high fees to have cellphones charged. Similar problems face military and law enforcement personnel. Modern soldiers, for example, head into the field carrying as much as 20 pounds of batteries to power communications equipment, laptop computers and night-vision goggles.

11　The energy generated by the footwear-embedded harvester can be used in one of two ways. It can be used directly to power a broad range of devices, from smartphones and laptops to radios, GPS units, night-vision goggles and flashlights.

12　Alternatively, the energy harvester can be integrated with a Wi-Fi hot spot that acts as a "middleman" between mobile devices and a wireless network. ④ <u>This allows users to seamlessly utilize the energy generated by the harvester without having to physically connect their mobile devices to the footwear.</u> Such a configuration dramatically reduces power consumption of wireless mobile devices and allows them to operate for much longer time without battery recharge, the Wisconsin researchers say.

13　"You cut the power requirements of your cellphone dramatically by doing this," says Krupenkin. "Your cellphone battery will last 10 times longer."

14　Even though energy harvesting is unlikely to completely replace batteries in the majority of mobile applications, the UW-Madison researchers believe it can play a key role in reducing cost, pollution and other problems associated with battery use. ⑤ <u>The hope, they say, is that the novel mechanical to electrical energy conversion process they pioneered can go a long way toward achieving that goal.</u>

(From *News of University of Wisconsin-Madison*, August 26, 2011)

Notes

[1] ***Nature Communications***: A peer-reviewed open access scientific journal published by the Nature Publishing Group since 2010. It covers the natural sciences, including physics, chemistry, Earth sciences, and biology. The journal has editorial offices in London, New York City, and Shanghai. Starting October 2014, the journal only accepted submissions from authors willing to pay an article processing charge, and until the end of 2015, part of the published submissions were only available to subscribers. In January 2016, all content became freely accessible to the public.

[2] **UW-Madison**: Short for University of Wisconsin-Madison.

Words and Phrases

sprint /sprɪnt/ *v.*

　run at full speed over a short distance　短跑；冲刺

substrate /ˈsʌbstreɪt/ *n.*

　an underlying substance or layer　基底；基质

seamlessly /ˈsiːmɪsli/ *adv.*

　smoothly and continuously, with no apparent gaps or spaces between one part and the next　无缝地

configuration /kənˌfɪɡəˈreɪʃn/ *n.*

　an arrangement of parts or elements in a particular form, figure, or combination　配置；构型

electrical grid

　an interconnected network for delivering electricity from suppliers to consumers. It consists of generating stations that produce electrical power, high-voltage transmission lines that carry power from distant sources to demand centers, and distribution lines that connect individual customers.　输电网络

Reading Comprehension Questions

1. What have Krupenkin and Taylor discovered? _____

   (A) Energy that humans produce when they walk.

   (B) Energy harvesting technology aimed at high-power applications.

   (C) Energy harvesting technology aimed at low-power applications.

   (D) Energy harvesting technology aimed at applications in the watts range.

2. In the first line of paragraph 7, the word "novel" means _____.

   (A) strange   (B) original

   (C) fictional   (D) great

3. According to the article, at what stage is this energy harvesting technology? _____

   (A) It has been developed.

   (B) It has been put into use.

   (C) It has been commercialized.

   (D) It is meeting great difficulties.

4. The limitations that current battery technology imposes on mobile electronics users are mentioned except that _____.

   (A) the utility of mobile electronic devices are greatly restricted

   (B) the facilities for recharging batteries are often not available

   (C) batteries in developing countries are expensive

   (D) batteries for some electronic equipment are heavy to carry

5. In the majority of mobile applications, energy harvesting will _____.

   (A) completely replace batteries

   (B) lead to a new type of battery

   (C) make batteries more powerful

   (D) reduce our dependence on batteries

(选文、注释:邹红云)

2. How Solar Can Save India's Farmers

By David Ferris

1 The solar farms[1] in India could save farmers from having to pay grand sums to fuel their water pumps.

2 Ravi Kant, a rice and wheat farmer in his 30s, lives in Bihar, just south of Nepal[2] and one of the poorest states in India. Kant used to perform an intricate ritual when rains alone couldn't provide enough water for his crops: He would rent a diesel pump from town, shoulder it on a bamboo sling and carry it to a corner of his property where he could drench one of his flat fields with water from an underground aquifer. Then he would move it to another quadrant, and another. "The discharge of water from the diesel pump was never strong," Kant recalled. "Add to that the time and hassle to rent a van, go to the town and buy diesel."

3 But life recently became much easier for Kant: His fertile acreage near the banks of the iconic river now has its own 7.5 horsepower water pump powered by six 6-foot-square solar panels. ① Watering his fields is as simple as walking a plastic hose past the huts where the women dry cow patties for stove fuel. When the sun shines, the farmer can summon water from the ground whenever he wants, and even on cloudy winter days he can irrigate for at least two hours.

4 A consensus is building that India needs millions more farmers who, like Kant, run their irrigation on sunshine. The country is home to 25 million agricultural water pumps, more than anywhere on earth. Whether they draw their power from the country's rickety power grid or from diesel-fueled generators, the pumps cause a host of problems. They are sucking aquifers dry, draining the government treasury and farmer's pockets, and adding to the

country's burgeoning carbon emissions levels.

5   A growing number of government officials, aid workers and entrepreneurs believe that if any sector is ripe for solar power in India, it is the legions of agricultural irrigation pumps, because the benefits could add up so quickly.

6   "In my view, India should stop doing all other solar and just focus on giving farmers a solution for their needs," said Pashupathy Gopalan, a managing director of SunEdison, an American firm that is one of India's largest developers of big solar farms and rooftop solar panels. "The farmers will be happy, and once the farmers are happy, the politicians will be happy because the farmer tells his family how to vote."

7   To know how a solar pumpset, as it's called, can make such a difference, it's worth taking a moment to understand the strange burden that watering crops places on the national electric grid. India's planning commission estimates that farming accounts for about 15 percent of gross domestic product (GDP) but the sector consumes some 25 percent of the nation's electricity, mostly from powering irrigation pumps. Utilities provide this power at a huge loss; electricity for farmers is usually free, or nearly so, costing only a couple of pennies per kilowatt.

8   It's been this way for decades, the legacy of a country that is quickly urbanizing but whose self-image and nearly 70 percent of its population is still rooted in the countryside. The policy comes at a high cost, both in energy and money. The power lines experience transmission losses of 30 to 40 percent on their long route to customers who pay almost nothing. "Every watt sold to a rural customer is a loss to the bottom line," explained Srinivasan Padmanaban, a senior energy adviser to the U.S. Agency for International Development (U.S.A.ID) in New Delhi.

9   ② <u>This burden is taking its toll on the rest of India. Most state electricity boards, the rough equivalent of U.S. utilities, are operating in the red, and the nation's power system frequently falters under the demand pressure of the fast-growing country.</u> In July 2012, more than half of India's population, 670

million people, experienced the world's largest blackout ever. Smaller, rolling blackouts are common, even in some of India's largest cities, spurred on by an outdated power grid, electricity theft, chronic shortages of fuel and the rising cost of imported coal and petroleum. Easing energy demand is a top priority.

10 And if the flickering power grid is a headache for utility officers and city dweller, it is an obstacle of another kind for the farmer, sometimes a deadly one. Farmers get electricity, but often for only a few hours a day or, rather, the night, when no other customers need it. This means that many farmers stumble out of bed and irrigate their fields in the dark. India is home to many venomous snakes like cobras and vipers, and it is fairly common, Gopalan said, for a farmer to meet his end with a snakebite.

11 These exhausted farmers who depend on short bursts of free electricity are not the best stewards of the nation's diminishing supply of groundwater. The system incentivizes the farmer to use as much water as he can when he can get it. Thus, many farmers gravitate toward crops that require flooding, like rice and wheat. But these commodities offer farmers the lowest of profit margins. Global consulting firm KPMG[3] estimates that solar pumps, which give a farmer the leisure to pump water only when he needs it, and can see it, could increase agricultural income by 10 to 15 percent by letting farmers switch to more profitable crops such as tomatoes and potatoes.

12 ③ <u>Converting all of India's electric water pumps to solar would appear to make imminent sense, but the economic argument for solar is even more compelling for diesel-powered pumps.</u> Solar-powered water pumps, which include a power source and expensive electronics, currently cost upwards of $6,000, whereas a pump that runs on electricity or diesel can be had for as little as $500. That's an enormous difference in a country with a per capita yearly income of only $1,200. farmers who get their electricity for free would probably rather save their money and risk the cobras. But for the 7 million diesel-using farmers like Kant, most of whom have no electrical connection and have had no choice but diesel pumps, they can spend up to 35 or 40 percent of

their income on diesel. And that amount is rising because the country is phasing out its subsidy on the fuel.

13 ④ Energy subsidies, however, aren't necessarily going away — they're instead moving toward solar. "We see a huge market for solar pumps in India," said G. Prasad, head of off-grid solar projects for the Indian Ministry of New and Renewable Energy, which is offering to pick up 30% of the cost of solar pumpsets. Ten states have also added their own subsidies. ⑤ Rural energy independence appeals to local politicians who can steer money to their constituents, as well as ministerial bean counters who see a potential for savings. KPMG estimates that if the government purchased 100,000 solar pumps, India could save $53 million a year in diesel imports.

14 The prospect of government largesse, combined with millions of potential customers, has global solar and pump manufacturers, from SunEdison to Germany's Lorentz to Denmark's Grundfos, running toward the Indian market. Kant's pump was installed by Claro Energy, an Indian startup that is competing with the big multinationals. "It's a tremendous opportunity because of the sheer size of the country, the sheer size of the population," said Melanie Natarajan, head of Asia-Pacific water operations for Franklin Electric, an American pump maker.

15 Ravi Kant couldn't be happier with his solar-powered pumps—not just because subsidies have driven his power costs down to zero. Instead of wrestling with a diesel-powered pump in front of his cows, he adjusts the panels a few times a day to point them toward the sun, and every few days washes the dust off. He said that he can grow one more crop now because of the solar pumps. He also said that his annual income is up to about 20,000 rupees (U.S. $347) per year.

16 Solar panels have been known to work for two decades and more. If they do, the blue-tinted solar panels will empower another generation — Kant's children — to water their own crops with sunshine.

(From Smithsonian. com, June 26, 2013)

Notes

[1] **Solar Farm**: a photovoltaic power station, especially when sited in agricultural areas, which is mostly built from hundreds or thousands of solar panels that generates and supplies solar electricity in commercial and residential applications.

[2] **Nepal**: a landlocked country located in South Asia. With an area of 147,181 square kilometers and a population of approximately 27 million, Nepal is the world's 93rd largest country by area and the 41st most populous country. It is located in the Himalayas and bordered to the north by China and to the south, east, and west by India. Kathmandu is the nation's capital city and largest metropolis.

[3] **KPMG**: a professional service company, being one of the Big Four auditors, along with Deloitte, EY and PwC. Seated in Amsterdam, Netherlands, KPMG employs 174,000 people and has three lines of services: audit, tax and advisory. Its tax and advisory services are further divided into various service groups.

Words and Phrases

ritual /ˈrɪtʃuəl/ *n.*

　　a series of actions that are always performed in the same way, especially as part of a religious ceremony 仪式

bamboo sling /ˌbæmˈbuːslɪŋ/ *n.*

　　a device like a bag for carrying things on a bamboo pole 竹挑子

aquifer /ˈækwɪfə(r)/ *n.*

　　a layer of rock or soil that can absorb and hold water 含水层

quadrant /ˈkwɒdrənt/ *n.*

　　(a kind of) rice field 水田

hassle /ˈhæsl/ n.

　a situation that is annoying because it involves doing sth. difficult or complicated that needs a lot of effort 困难；麻烦

iconic /aɪˈkɒnɪk/ adj.

　acting as a sign or symbol of sth. 标致性的

cow patty /kaʊˈpæti/ n.

　cow shit 牛粪

consensus /kənˈsensəs/ n.

　an opinion that all members of a group agree with 共识

rickety /ˈrɪkəti/ adj.

　not strong, easy to break or in bad condition 不稳定的

burgeoning /ˈbɜːdʒənɪŋ/ adj.

　quickly growing or developing 急剧增长的

sector /ˈsektə(r)/ n.

　a part of an area of activity, especially of a country's economy 领域；行业

falter /ˈfɔltə(r)/ v.

　to become weaker or unable to continue in an effective way 工作不稳定

rolling /ˈrəʊlɪŋ/ adj.

　done at regular intervals over a period of time 周而复始的

flickering /ˈflɪkərɪŋ/ adj.

　done in an unsteady way 不稳定的

venomous /ˈvenəməs/ adj.

　producing venom 分泌毒液的；有毒的

steward /ˈstjuːəd/ n.

　a person employed to manage another person's property or take care of passengers 管家；乘务员

incentivize /ɪnˈsentɪvaɪz/ v.

　to encourage sb. to behave in a particular way by offering them a reward 激励；奖励

gravitate /ˈɡrævɪteɪt/ v.

to move towards sb./sth. that you are attracted to 被吸引

per capita /pəˈkæpɪtə/ *adj.*

for each person 人均的

constituent /kənˈstɪtʃuənt/ *n.*

a person who lives, and can vote in a district 选民

largesse /lɑːˈdʒes/ *n.*

the act or quality of being generous with money 慷慨的赠与；施舍

startup /ˈstɑːtʌp/ *n.*

a company that is just beginning to operate 刚成立的公司；新企业

power grid

the network of electricity supply 电网

in the red

owing more than you have; in debt 负债

phase out

to gradually stop using or providing sth. 逐步取消

bean counter

a person who works with money and wants to keep strict control of how much money a company spends 精打细算的账房先生

Reading Comprehension Questions

1. Watering crops is a burden on India's national power grid for all of the reasons except _____.

    (A) running water pumps consumes a lot of electricity

    (B) farmers have a free supply of electricity

    (C) India is experiencing rapid urbanization

    (D) 30 percent to 40 percent of electricity is lost on transmission

2. The policy to give farmers free electricity creates problems because _____.

(A) it is taking its toll on the rest of India

(B) it places a burden on the country in terms of energy and money

(C) it discourages people from moving to cities

(D) India still uses an outdated power grid

3. According to the passage, if farmers want to increase their agricultural income, they need to _____.

   (A) install rooftop solar panels

   (B) help build a power grid

   (C) grow rice and wheat

   (D) grow tomatoes and potatoes

4. It can be inferred from the passage that _____.

   (A) farmers get money from the government for their use of diesel

   (B) farmers replace pumps that run on electricity or diesel with solar-powered ones

   (C) farmers don't see a good market for solar pumps in the future

   (D) farmers want their children to enjoy the urban life

5. The author shares the opinion that India will be a huge solar market because _____.

   (A) people don't want any more blackouts

   (B) the government is generous in its subsidy on the fuel

   (C) millions of people will switch to the use of solar power

   (D) international solar manufacturers can't find anywhere else to make more money than in India

(选文、注释:薛光荣)

3. Is the Mobile Phone a Blessing or a Curse?

By Neil Gordon

1   "I can't live without my mobile phone!" is what I often hear people say as they lament about how mobiles have become an indispensable part of their lives. The blurring of personal and work lives brought about by the device are posing challenges to many.

2   The all so common sight of heads bent, eyes staring intently at mobile screens and fingers busy tapping away repeats itself across major cities around the world. Whenever there is a moment to spare while on the train, taxi or waiting in a queue, people busy themselves with their mobile devices. Some even confess to checking in with their phones while out on a date!

3   ① <u>Such unhealthy obsession with mobile devices is disrupting how we appreciate the little things in life or miss the moments that matter. The truth is that technology overall should be seen as a tool to enhance our way of living and not as a backfill for the good things that we as humans naturally enjoy.</u>

4   Mobile phones have certainly made a significant impact on our lives, but I truly believe it's for the better.

5   It's changed the way we communicate, whether for work or play. We are now less constrained by time and geographical location. ② <u>With my mobile device, I can dial into conference calls while stuck in a traffic jam, or reply to urgent e-mails while on the go. I can send a text message or share photos and videos with friends who aren't living in the same country.</u> My phone calendar keeps my life organised, and even Facebook, Twitter, and instant messaging are now accessible from mobile devices!

6   Smartphones are more than just a means to stay connected; they are also a

key source of entertainment. ③ The game of Snake[1] was one of the first mobile games that I got hooked on way back in the 1990s. Today, the market's flooded with mobile apps — we're so spoilt for choice! And it's not just games. There are apps to help you find your way around literally anywhere, apps that let you listen to your favourite music, apps to book cinema or concert tickets, and even apps that teach the alphabet to toddlers.

7   The mobile revolution isn't just changing the lives of urbanites like myself. I know of a young Bangladeshi woman named Shompa Akhter who has a passion for fashion and design. She dreamt about starting her own business and she did just that, opening a boutique in Kushtia featuring her own creations. Dealing with suppliers in different towns was a hassle for Shompa — purchase orders had to either be hand delivered or mailed out to suppliers. Shompa also found it tough publicizing her business to potential customers outside her town.

8   ④ Before using a mobile phone, Shompa had never heard of e-mails! The technology intimidated her and she was sceptical about how a mobile phone and e-mail could help her business. But once she got the hang of it, she was hooked. Mobile e-mail is a blessing in her life. The 25-year-old entrepreneur now stays in touch easily with her suppliers.

9   I hear inspiring stories like Shompa's from so many other countries. Teachers, like Edna Cas and Imelda Pontejos from Ligao East Central School in the Philippines, have brought lessons to life in the classrooms by downloading multimedia content via smartphones using the Text2Teach programme[2] and linking it to television screens to show to their students.

10   ⑤ Farmers, like Edi Sugara Purba in North Sumatra, Indonesia now have access to weather information critical to crops. With the information gained through his mobile phone, Edi can quickly decide how to best protect the coffee and oranges he grows. He also gets information on crop prices to help him negotiate better and decide on how to price his crops competitively.

11   Who would have thought that mobility could effect such monumental

change? It shouldn't really be a surprise though. Information is empowering. Just ask Shompa, Edna and Edi.

12   Still, close to 6 billion mobile phone users don't own a smartphone. Another 3.2 billion people don't own a mobile device at all. The mobile revolution is here but there are still many out there who have yet to experience its benefits. We've only just begun.

(From *Reader's Digest*, http://readersdigest. com. au/true-stories-lifestyle/science-technology/mobile-phone-blessing-or-curse.)

Notes

[1] **The Game of Snake**: a game where the player maneuvers a line which grows in length, with the line itself being a primary obstacle. There is no standard version of the game. The concept originated in the 1976 arcade game Blockade, and its simplicity has led to many implementations (some of which have the word snake or worm in the title). After a variant was preloaded on Nokia mobile phones in 1998, there was a resurgence of interest in the Snake concept as it found a larger audience.

[2] **Text2Teach Programme**: a mobile learning package which uses a smartphone and a specialized SIM card to download comprehensive educational videos of Math, Science, English, and Values Education subjects for 5th and 6th grade students. It utilizes Globe Telecom's mobile network to allow teachers even in remote areas to access educational materials to supplement their lessons. It was recognized as one of the exemplary Information Communications Technology (ICT) innovations for education in the recent "Asia-Pacific Ministerial Forum on ICT in Education (AMFIE) 2013" in China.

Words and Phrases

blur /blɜː(r)/   v.

(cause sth. to) become unclear or indistinct 使某事物变得模糊不清

constrain /kənˈstren/ v.

make sb. do sth. by force 强迫某人做某事

urbanity /ɜːˈbænəti/ n.

refined manner and smooth elegance 温雅有礼

intimidate /ɪnˈtɪmɪdeɪt/ v.

to frighten sb. in order to make him do sth. 恐吓、威胁某人做某事

entrepreneur /ˌɒntrəprəˈnɜː(r)/ n.

person who starts or organizes a commercial enterprise 企业家

negotiate /nɪˈɡəʊʃɪeɪt/ v.

try to reach agreement by discussion 商议;谈判

slip up

make a careless mistake 出差错

lament about

complain about 抱怨

sceptical about

unwilling to believe sth. 不肯相信的

get the hang of

learn how to operate or do sth. 熟悉某物的用法

Suggested Topics for Writing

1. Some people believe that the mobile phone is a blessing. Others believe that it is a curse. Which point of view do you agree with? Use specific reasons and details to explain your answer.

2. Do you agree or disagree with the following statement "The mobile phone can disrupt how we appreciate the little things in life or miss the moments that matter"? Use specific reasons and examples to support your opinion.

(选文:任爱军;注释:马仁蓉)

Unit Seven   Medical World

1. Why We Should Study Cancer Like We Study Ecosystems

By Rachel Nuwer

1   When pine beetles invaded North American forests, they threw a delicate ecosystem out of balance. Cancer cells, too, behave like damaging invasive species.

2   Sometimes, thinking about an old problem from a refreshing new angle is just the thing needed to find that eureka[1] moment.

3   Cancer, one of the most notorious medical maladies, has been studied intensely in the current era of modern medicine. But a growing number of researchers think that bringing a fresh, out-of-the-box approach to understanding the disease may lead to some novel insights and, perhaps, solutions. And the subject that they're hoping can serve as a window into the study of cancer may surprise you: ecology.

4   On face value, oncology and ecology seem vastly different. For example, one is localized to specific cells in the body, while the other by definition spans the entire globe. But rather than labeling cancer as a group of mutated cells, as the thinking goes, we should see cancer as a disruption in the balance of a complex microenvironment in the human body. ① Like a damaging invasive

beetle eating its way through forests in Colorado, a novel disease breaking out in populations of wild birds, or loggers mowing down parts of the Amazon rainforest, cancer throws a monkey wrench into an otherwise placid, balanced system.

5   This way of thinking makes cancer seem even more complex than it already is, but it could provide insights that ultimately make cancer more treatable, propose researchers from the Moffet Cancer Center in a paper published in the journal *Interface Focus*.

6   "Einstein is known to have said that everything should be made as simple as possible, but not simpler," they write. ② "It turns out that complexity has its place and, as convenient as it would be for cancer biologists to study tumor cells in isolation, that makes as much sense as trying to understand frogs without considering that they tend to live near swamps and feast on insects."

7   We tend to think of cancer only in terms of mutated cells, the authors continue. But adopting this narrow approach is like trying to understand why a frog has a sticky tongue without taking into account that frogs use their tongues to catch insects. Cancer cells, likewise, need context. A voracious cancer cell, for example, may situate itself next to a blood vessel not by chance, but by choice so it can obtain more nutrients and oxygen to support its unlimited division.

8   Cancer cells must compete within the body for nutrients and other resources, just like animals living in an environment must compete with one another in order to survive. This means that cancer, like any organism, must adapt to its environment in order to thrive. The researchers explain:

It is now beginning to be widely accepted that cancer is not just a genetic disease but the one in which evolution plays a crucial role. This means that tumor cells evolve, adapt to and change the environment in which they live. The ones that fail to do so will ultimately become extinct. The ones that do will have a chance to invade and metastasize.

③ *The capacity of a tumor cell to adapt to a new environment will thus be determined by environment and the cellular species from the original site, to which it has already painstakingly adapted.*

9   So how can all of this theory be applied in real life? The environmental approach to understanding cancer is so complex that it rules out normal experiments; they could easily go away with so many different components to consider. Instead, the researchers suggest turning to mathematics and computation for understanding the greater environmental context that leads to cancer. Ecologists use one such mathematical approach, game theory[2], as a way to study evolutionary biology and the way animals interact:

The force of natural selection keeps ecosystem denizens focused on optimizing the bottom line: long-term reproduction. In the games studied by evolutionary game theoreticians, individuals compete for available resources using a variety of strategies. These features and behaviors, known as the phenotypic strategy, determine the winners and losers of evolution.

10   Behavioral strategies may change depending upon both an animal's nature and the situation's context. Here's a hypothetical example, based upon game theory thinking: If two hyenas are digging into a large, tasty wild beast carcass, they'll happily share that resource. But if two lions find that same carcass, they will fight for exclusive rights to eating it, meaning one lion emerges victorious and takes all the meaty spoils, while the other gets no food or even gets injured. Finally, if a lion meets a hyena at the carcass, the hyena will bolt, surrendering its goods to the stronger lion. In other words, game theory players can react one of the three ways depending upon who they are and what's going on: they can share, fight or forfeit.

11   Similar games may be played with tumor cells. "A good example would be a tumor with cells that move away when confronted with scarce resources and cells that stay to use them," the authors write. To make things even more complicated, however, tumor cells are known to change their behavior as they proliferate and metastasize throughout the body, meaning they could switch

from a hyena to a lion.

12 One crucial thing that game theory at an ecosystem level shows us, they continue, is that indiscriminately focusing on killing as many tumor cells as possible might not provide the best outcome for the patient. According to game theory models, the eventual long-term result of the game depends upon specific interactions between the players, not on the number of players involved. Lions will continue to fight one another for food, regardless of whether two lions or 2,000 lions meet. "A treatment based exclusively on indiscriminately removing most (but not all) cancer cells may only have a temporary effect; as in most cases, the original number of tumor cells will eventually be restored and exceeded," the authors write.

13 Instead, game theory indicates that a more effective alternative would be based on trying to change the ways that cells interact with one another and with their environment. This may affect the cells' behavior, strength and reproductive success, the authors explain, which could drive a tumor's evolution towards less aggressive cell types, or to a more stable coexistence with non-cancerous cells.

14 "The ecosystem view is, ultimately, a holistic[3] one that sees cancer progression as a process that emerges from the interactions between multiple cellular species and interactions with the tumor microenvironment," the authors write. ④ "An ecosystem perspective presents us with intriguing implications," they say, along with a host of questions about how far the analogy between ecosystem and cancer can be taken.

15 For example, if cancer cells spread like an invasive species through an ecosystem, what evolutionary gain is achieved when the closed off ecosystem (a body) is irreparably damaged (through a person's death) such that the pestilence also dies? Unlike a virus, which may kill its host but spread to other hosts in the process, cancer cells themselves, for the most part, have no means of spreading from individual to individual. And are cancer cells taking their cues from processes driven by competition or from cooperation? Thinking more

proactively, can non-cancerous cells be triggered so that they behave like lions and usurp cancerous cells' resources until the cancer is manageable?

16   While ecology and mathematics likely will not defeat cancer on their own, viewing the disease from this perspective could allow doctors to better predict where in the body tumor cells have the best and worst chances of survival, and how to most effectively prevent them from proliferating.

17   ⑤ "The heart of the matter is that an ecological view of tumors does not invalidate but complements and builds upon decades of cancer research and undoubtedly this will lead to a better understanding of the biology of cancer and to new and improved therapies," the researchers conclude. "We need to properly understand the trees (e.g., every leaf, twig and branch) before we can understand the forest but we cannot afford to ignore the forest because the trees are so interesting on their own."

(From Smithsonian.com, June 24, 2013)

Notes

[1] **Eureka**: A cry of joy or satisfaction when one finds or discovers something. The word came from Greek "*heurēka*" (I have found it), said to have been uttered by Archimedes when he hit upon a method of determining the purity of gold.

[2] **Game Theory(博弈论)**: The branch of mathematics concerned with the analysis of strategies for dealing with competitive situations where the outcome of a participant's choice of action depends critically on the actions of other participants. Game theory has been applied to contexts in war, business, and biology.

[3] **Holism(整体主义;整体论)**: The belief that everything in nature is connected in some way.

Words and Phrases

oncology /ɒŋˈkɒlədʒɪ/ *n.*

the study and treatment of tumours 肿瘤学

voracious /vəˈreɪʃəs/ *adj.*

wanting or devouring great quantities of food 贪吃的

metastasize /məˈtæstəsaɪz/ *v.*

(of a cancer) spread to other sites in the body （癌细胞）扩散

denizen /ˈdenɪzn/ *n.*

a person, animal, or plant that lives or is found in a particular place 生活在特定地方的人（动物或植物）

forfeit /ˈfɔːfɪt/ *v.*

lose or be deprived of (property or a right or privilege) as a penalty for wrongdoing 失去；被迫放弃

pestilence /ˈpestɪləns/ *n.*

any disease that spreads quickly and kills large numbers of people 瘟疫

usurp /juːˈzɜːp/ *v.*

seize and take control without authority and possibly with force 篡夺；夺取

Reading Comprehension Questions

1. The expression "throws a monkey wrench into" (line 7, paragraph 4) most probably means _____.

   (A) opens a window into

   (B) brings a change to

   (C) causes a problem to

   (D) develops a theory of

2. According to the passage, the winners and losers of evolution are determined

by their ability to _____.

(A) use plenty of behavioral strategies

(B) outsmart their natural enemies

(C) get access to available resources

(D) take advantage of their living environment

3. From the passage we know that tumor cells could be better handled by _____.

(A) keeping them off from normal surrounding cells

(B) weakening their power for aggressive behavior

(C) cutting off the supply of nutrients for their growth

(D) changing how cells interact with each other and with their environment

4. An ecological view of tumors might serve as a window into the study of cancer because _____.

(A) it could help doctors see better how tumor cells survive and develop in human bodies

(B) it could give doctors a chance to find out more about how tumor cells interact with non-cancerous cells

(C) it could reveal how closely the environment in which we live is related with the microenvironment in human bodies

(D) it could lead to a better understanding of the interaction between people and tumors

5. According to the passage, all of the following statements are true except _____.

(A) invasive species like pine beetles causes damage to North American forests

(B) it is not right to view cancer as a disruption in the balance of a complex microenvironment in the human body

(C) animals behave differently according to their nature and different situations

(D) a virus spreads to other hosts after killing its host

(选文:薛光荣;注释:邹红云)

2. Three Ways Video Games Can Improve Health Care

By Pete Etchells

1   I was a gamer kid. Heck, I still am a gamer kid. And like any form of media, old or new, video games have had their fair share of negative airtime. Much like how comic books were vilified in the 1950s for corroding young and impressionable minds (although the research behind those claims is now in dispute), video games are similarly being scrutinized for their effects on development and behavior.

2   But a relatively new branch of science is focusing on the therapeutic aspects of video games. This new generation of researchers who have grown up with video games are starting to use their unique mix of skills to look into the possibility of improving people's lives through gaming. And there's three promising areas where games appear to have a unique leg up on traditional therapies.

(1) Focusing Attention

3   A study released today finds that video games can be therapeutic in what first seems like an unlikely context: treating dyslexia. Researchers tested the reading and attentional skills of kids with dyslexia before and after playing video games over the course of nine separate 80-minute sessions. They found that action video games, specifically, left the kids able to read faster and better able to focus their attention. In fact, those 12 total hours of video games play did just as much, or more, for reading skills than demanding traditional reading therapies.

4   Attention and reading skills probably go hand in hand, the researchers say. ① "Visual attention deficits are surprisingly way more predictive of future

reading disorders than are language abilities at the prereading stage," said study author Andrea Facoetti of the University of Padua in Italy. By improving visual attention, then, games can address this root cause of dyslexia.

5   A different kind of attention control can be useful for combating pain. Back in 2003, researchers at the University of Washington's HITLab developed a new virtual reality game called SnowWorld to help patients with severe burns. The game is built on the idea that pain competes with other mental stimuli for our limited amount of attention. In SnowWorld, players move around an environment full of things like penguins, snowmen and woolly mammoths, which they have to shoot with snowballs, and all the while, Paul Simon[1] songs are playing in the background. So much is going on that patients haven't got much attentional capacity left over to think about anything else. And because they can't devote any resources to thinking about their burns, amazingly, they report feeling less pain.

(2) **Providing a Story**

6   "Video games have some really important elements that make them great learning tools," says Elisabeth Whyte, a researcher in the Developmental Neuroscience lab at Penn State University who also runs the extremely successful Restokin World of Warcraft[2] blog. "They provide much more than just a feedback and reward system. Game-based elements also include a storyline and plot, which can provide a motivation and reasoning for why you are doing that behavior."

7   Whyte is working on a project that will develop game-based interventions for individuals with autism. ② <u>By helping to improve abilities such as making eye contact with other people and understanding emotional expressions in faces, the hope is that games will help autistic individuals to improve their interpersonal skills.</u>

8   Without story, game-based therapies are very often incredibly dry. "Most existing interventions tend to stick the reward piece from games onto existing tasks that are boring and repetitive, but they don't really have a plot and

storyline," explains Elisabeth. For example, imagine a task in which you're shown a scene, and you have to identify what a person in the scene is feeling—maybe they look sad. If you correctly complete the trial, you get a reward in the shape of positive feedback ("Well done! You earned 10 points!"). The problem is that tasks like this often involve a large number of repeated trials, and by the time a participant gets to the end, the game has lost all meaning—who cares if the girl is sad or not, anyway?

9 So instead, imagine a game in which the task is the same as before, but it's now couched within a detective story. When you correctly identify what emotion the character is feeling, the person gets logged as a witness in a case investigating a bank robbery. Once you correctly identify 10 witnesses, you arrest the thief, and for every 10 crooks you apprehend, you get promoted.

10 Rethinking the way in which experimental tasks are presented is simple yet effective, and it's Elisabeth's background as a gamer that has helped her develop this insight. ③ <u>"It draws on really important elements of game design that aren't obvious unless you've played games such as World of Warcraft and have an understanding of what drives people to spend seven or more years of their life playing this type of role-playing game,"</u> she says.

(3) **Doing Battle**

11 Finally, that very violence people decry about video games may in itself have some positive applications—for instance, in battling cancer.

12 The third-person shooter gamere-Mission was developed by non-profit organization HopeLab in 2006 to help teenagers with cancer. In the game players control a friendly humanoid called Roxxi who flies through the bloodstream of a variety of teen characters suffering from the disease. Roxxi battles bacteria with her built-in gun, doses medication to recalcitrant teens, and blasts cancerous cells.

13 Along the way, players learn about lots of different aspects of cancer that can be quite scary—chemotherapy, taking antibiotics, techniques to prevent mucositis, and so on—in a completely non-threatening environment. ④ <u>In a</u>

2008 randomized controlled trial looking at the effectiveness of the game, researchers found that players not only knew more about cancer, but were more likely to keep up with their chemotherapy and antibiotic treatments. In other words, including video game play had a hugely positive impact on factors relating to their survival.

14 So, like anything in science, the story of how video games affect us is a complex one. Yes, there are issues concerning problematic gaming use, and the question of whether violent video games have negative effects on behavior is still under intense debate. ⑤ As a result, it's easy to lose sight of the fact that "video game" isn't a one-dimensional entity—and that games can be a force for good, significantly improving the lives of people with diseases in brave new ways.

(From *Discover*, February 28, 2013)

Notes

[1] **Paul Simon**: Born on October 13, 1941 in Newark New Jersey, Paul Simon is one of the most successful and respected singer/songwriters of the second half of the 20th century. Rising to fame in the mid-1960s, Simon's songs were mature and literate, but also melodically engaging, and spoke to the concerns and uncertainties of a generation.

[2] **World of Warcraft**: Commonly known as WoW, is a pay-to-play massively multiplayer online role-playing game. The game was released on November 23, 2004, celebrating the 10th anniversary of the Warcraft franchise.

Words and Phrases

heck /hek/ *inj.*

used to show that you are slightly annoyed or surprised 表示略微烦恼或吃惊

airtime /ˈeətaɪm/ n.

the amount of time that is given to a particular subject on radio or television 播放时间

vilify /ˈvɪlɪfaɪ/ v.

to say or write unpleasant things about sb./sth. so that other people will have a low opinion of them 污蔑

corrode /kəˈrəʊd/ v.

to destroy sth. slowly 腐蚀

scrutinize /ˈskruːtənaɪz/ v.

to look at or examine sb./sth. carefully 仔细查看

dyslexia /dɪsˈleksiə/ n.

a slight disorder of brain that causes difficulty in reading and spelling, but does not affect intelligence 诵读困难

deficit /ˈdefɪsɪt/ n.

the amount by which sth., especially an amount of money, is too small or smaller than sth. else 不足额

stimulus /ˈstɪmjələs/ n.

(pl. stimuli) something that helps sb./sth. to develop better or more quickly 刺激物

mammoth /ˈmæməθ/ n.

an animal like a large elephant covered with hair, that lived thousands of years ago 猛犸象

blog /blɒg/ n.

a website where a person writes regularly about recent events or topics that interest them, usually with photos and links to other websites that they find interesting 博客

intervene /ˌɪntəˈviːn/ v.

to become involved in a situation in order to improve or help it 出面；介入

autism /ˈɔːtɪzəm/ n.

a mental condition in which a person finds it very difficult to communicate or form relationships with others 自闭症

couch /kaʊtʃ/ *v.*

to say or write words in a particular style or manner 表达

log /lɔg/ *v.*

to record 记录；登记

crook /krʊk/ *n.*

a dishonest person 骗子

apprehend /ˌæprɪˈhɛnd/ *v.*

to catch sb. and arrest him/her 逮捕

decry /dɪˈkraɪ/ *v.*

to strongly criticize sb./sth., especially publicly 公开谴责

humanoid /ˈhjʊməˈnɔɪd/ *n.*

a machine or creature that looks and behaves like a human 仿真机器人

recalcitrant /rɪˈkælsɪtrənt/ *adj.*

difficult to control 桀骜不驯的

chemotherapy /ˌkiːməʊˈθerəpi/ *n.*

the treatment of disease, especially cancer, with the use of chemical substances 化疗

antibiotic /ˌæntɪbaɪˈɒtɪk/ *n.*

a substance, for example penicillin, that can destroy or prevent the growth of bacteria, and cure infections 抗生素

mucositis /ˈmjuːkəsaɪtɪs/ *n.*

an inflammation of mucous membrane 黏膜炎

entity /ˈentəti/ *n.*

something that exists separately from other things and has its own identity 独立存在物

Reading Comprehension Questions

1. The main reason why video games can help treat dyslexia is _____.

    (A) they improve visual attention

    (B) they design interesting stories

    (C) they provide instruction in language abilities

    (D) they limit mental stimuli

2. In what way the game-based interventions developed by Whyte are effective for individuals with autism? _____

    (A) They help the individuals forget their illness.

    (B) They provide a feedback and reward system.

    (C) They have a plot and storyline.

    (D) They are simple.

3. By playing video games, teenagers with cancer _____.

    (A) feel less pain

    (B) understand emotional expressions better

    (C) learn more about cancer and be more positive in their treatments

    (D) devote much attention capacity to improve their interpersonal relation

4. We can conclude from the article that _____.

    (A) researches have shown that comic books will not corrode the young and impressionable minds

    (B) visual attention deficits are more likely to result in reading disorders than are problems with language abilities at the prereading stage

    (C) the therapeutic aspects of video games have made them replace traditional therapies

    (D) violent video games have negative effects on development and behavior

5. What is the writer's attitude toward video games? _____

    (A) Ambivalent.   (B) Cautious.

    (C) Objective.   (D) Vague.

(选文、注释:陈静)

3. Yes, Don't Impede Medical Progress

By Virginia Postrel[1]

1   To many biologists, the recently announced creation of a cloned human embryo was no big deal. True, researchers at Advanced Cell Technology (ACT)[2] replaced the nucleus of a human egg with the genetic material of another person. And they got that cloned cell to start replicating. But their results were modest. It took seventy-one eggs to produce a single success, and in the best case, the embryo grew to only six cells before dying. That's not a revolution. It's an incremental step in understanding how early-stage cells develop.

2   ① And it's far from the one hundred or so cells in a blastocyst, the hollow ball from which stem cells can be isolated. Scientists hope to coax embryonic stem cells into becoming specialized tissues such as nerve, muscle, or pancreatic islet cells. Therapeutic cloning, or nucleus transplantation, could make such treatments more effective.

3   In theory, it would work like this: Suppose I need new heart tissue or some insulin-secreting islet cells to counteract diabetes. You could take the nucleus from one of my cells, stick it in an egg cell from which the nucleus had been removed, let that develop into stem cells, and then trigger the stem cells to form the specific tissue needed. The new "cloned" tissue would be genetically mine and would not face rejection problems. It would function in my body as if it had grown there naturally, so I wouldn't face a lifetime of immunosuppressant drugs.

4   ② But all of that is a long way off. ACT and others in the field are still doing very basic research, not developing clinical therapies. Indeed, because of the difficulty of obtaining eggs, therapeutic cloning may ultimately prove

impractical for clinical treatments. It could be more important as a technique for understanding cell development or studying the mutations that lead to cancer. We simply don't know right now. Science is about exploring the unknown and cannot offer guarantees.

5   Politics, however, feeds on fear, uncertainty, and doubt, and the word "cloning" arouses those emotions. ③ <u>While its scientific importance remains to be seen, ACT's announcement had rekindled the campaign to criminalize nucleus transplantation and any therapies derived from that process. Under a bill passed by the House and endorsed by the president, scientists who transfer a human nucleus into an egg cell would be subject to ten-year federal prison sentences and $1 million fines.</u> So would anyone who imports therapies developed through such research in countries where it is legal, such as Britain. The bill represents an unprecedented attempt to criminalize basic biomedical research.

6   The legislation's backers consider the fear of cloning their best hope for stopping medical research that might lead to gene-level therapies. Opponents make three basic arguments for banning therapeutic cloning.

7   The first is that a fertilized egg is a person, entitled to full human rights. Taking stem cells out of a blastocyst is, in this view, no different from cutting the heart out of a baby. Hence, we hear fears of "embryo farming" for "spare parts".

8   ④ <u>This view treats microscopic cells with no past or present consciousness, no organs or tissues, as people. A vocal minority of Americans, of course, do find compelling the argument that a fertilized egg is someone who deserves protection from harm. That view animates the anti-abortion movement and exercises considerable influence in Republican politics.</u>

9   But most Americans don't believe we should sacrifice the lives and well-being of actual people to save cells. Human identity must rest on something more compelling than the right string of proteins in a Petri dish[3], detectable only with high-tech equipment. We will never get a moral consensus that a

single cell, or a clump of one hundred cells, is a human being. That definition defies moral sense, rational argument, and several major religious traditions.

10 So cloning opponents add a second argument. If we allow therapeutic cloning, they say, some unscrupulous person will pretend to be doing cellular research but instead implant a cloned embryo in a woman's womb and produce a baby. At the current stage of knowledge, using cloning to conceive a child would indeed be dangerous and unethical, with a high risk of serious birth defects. Anyone who cloned a baby today would rightly face, at the very least, the potential of an enormous malpractice judgment. There are good arguments for establishing a temporary moratorium on reproductive cloning.

11 ⑤ But the small possibility of reproductive cloning does not justify making nucleus transfer a crime. Almost any science might conceivably be turned to evil purposes. This particular misuse is neither especially likely — cell biology labs are not set up to deliver fertility treatments—nor, in the long run, especially threatening.

12 Contrary to a lot of scary rhetoric, a healthy cloned infant would not be a moral nightmare, merely the not-quite-identical twin of an older person. (The fetal environment and egg cytoplasm create some genetic variations.) Certainly, some parents might have such a baby for bad reasons, to gratify their egos or to "replace" a child who died. But parents have been having children for bad reasons since time immemorial.

13 Just as likely, cloned babies would be the cherished children of couples who could not have biological offspring any other way. These children might bear an uncanny resemblance to their biological parents, but that, too, is not unprecedented. Like the "test tube babies" born of in vitro fertilization, cloned children need not be identifiable, much less freaks or outcasts.

14 Why worry so much about a few babies? Because, say opponents, even a single cloned infant puts us on the road to genetic dystopia, a combination of Brave New World and Nazi Germany. A cloned child's genetic makeup is too well known, goes the argument, and therefore transforms random reproduction

into "manufacturing" that robs the child of his autonomy. This is where the attack broadens from nucleus transfer to human genetic engineering more generally. An anti-therapeutic cloning petition, circulated by the unlikely duo of conservative publisher William Kristol and arch-technophobe Jeremy Rifkin, concludes "We are mindful of the tragic history of social eugenics movements in the first half of the 20th century, and are united in our opposition to any use of biotechnology for a commercial eugenics movement in the 21st century."

15 But the "eugenics" they attack has nothing to do with state-sponsored mass murder or forced sterilization. To the contrary, they are the ones who want the state to dictate the most private aspects of family life. They are the ones who want central authorities, rather than the choices of families and individuals, to determine our genetic future. They are the ones who demand that the government control the means of reproduction. They are the ones who measure the worth of human beings by the circumstances of their conception and their purity of their genetic makeup. They are the ones who say "natural" genes are the mark of true humanity.

16 Winners in the genetic lottery themselves, blessed with good health and unusual intelligence, they seek to deny future parents the chance to give their children an equally promising genetic start.

17 Biomedicine does have the potential to alter the human experience. Indeed, it already has. Life expectancy has doubled worldwide in the past century. Childbirth is no longer a peril to mother and infant. Childhood is no longer a time for early death. The pervasive sense of mortality that down through the ages shaped art, religion, and culture has waned.

18 Our lives are different from our ancestors in fundamental ways. We rarely remark on the change, however, because it occurred incrementally. That's how culture evolves and how science works. We should let the process continue.

(From *The Wall Street Journal*, December 5, 2001)

Notes

[1] **Verginia Postrel**: Graduated with a degree in English from Princeton University, she was the editor of *Reason Magazine* from 1988 to 2000 and received the Free Press Association's Mencken Award for Commentary based on her editorials. More recently she has been writing the economic scene column for *the New York Times* business section. In this article, she argues that we should not get in the way of scientific progress.

[2] **Advanced Cell Technology (ACT)**: It is a biotechnology company located in Marlborough, Massachusetts, U.S.A.. The company specializes in the development and commercialization of cell therapies for the treatment of a variety of diseases.

[3] **Petri Dish**: Named after the German bacteriologist Julius Richard Petri, it is a shallow cylindrical glass or plastic lidded dish that biologists use to culture cells, such as bacteria or small mosses.

Words and Phrases

impede /ɪmˈpiːd/ v.

to delay or stop the progress of sth. 阻碍；阻止

incremental /ˌɪŋkrəˈmentl/ adj.

increasing in amount or value gradually and regularly 增长的

pancreatic islet /ˌpæŋkriˈætɪkˈaɪlət/ n.

the region of the pancreas that contain its hormone-producing cells 胰岛

insulin /ˈɪnsəlɪn/ n.

a chemical substance produced in the body that controls the amount of blood sugar 胰岛素

secrete /sɪˈkriːt/ v.

to produce a liquid substance 分泌

immunosuppressant /ˌɪmjunəʊsəˈpresənt/ *adj.*

stopping the body from reacting against antigens, e.g. in order to prevent the body from rejecting a new organ 免疫抑制的

mutation /mjuːˈteɪʃn/ *n.*

a process in which the genetic material of a person, an animal or a plant changes in structure when it is passed on to children, etc., causing different physical characteristics to develop 突变；变异

criminalize /ˈkrɪmɪnəlaɪz/ *v.*

to make sth. illegal by passing a new law 使不合法；使非法

fertilize /ˈfɜːtəlaɪz/ *v.*

to join sperm with an egg so that a baby or young animal develops 使受精

vocal /ˈvəʊkl/ *adj.*

telling people your opinions or protesting about sth. loudly and confidently 大声表达的；直言不讳的

animate /ˈænɪmeɪt/ *v.*

to make sth. more lively or full of energy 使有活力；使生气勃勃

clump /klʌmp/ *n.*

a small group of things or people very close together 群；组；簇

conceive /kənˈsiːv/ *v.*

to make a woman become pregnant 使怀上孩子

malpractice /ˌmælˈpræktɪs/ *n.*

careless, wrong or illegal behavior while in a professional job 渎职；玩忽职守

moratorium /ˌmɒrəˈtɔːriəm/ *n.*

a temporary stopping of an activity 暂停；中止

cytoplasm /ˈsaɪtəʊplæzəm/ *n.*

all the living material in a cell, not including the nucleus 细胞质

gratify /ˈɡrætɪfaɪ/ *v.*

to satisfy a wish, need, etc. 满足

immemorial /ˌɪməˈmɔːriəl/ *adj.*

that has existed for longer than people can remember 古老的；远古的

uncanny /ʌnˈkæni/ *adj*.

strange and difficult to explain 异常的；不可思议的

freak /fri:k/ *n*.

a person considered to be unusual because of the way he/she behaves, looks or thinks 怪异的人

duo /ˈdjuːəʊ/ *n*.

two people who perform together or are often seen together 搭档

arch-technophobe /ɑːtʃˈteknəʊfəʊb/ *n*.

a person who is so afraid of, dislikes new technology 非常害怕或厌恶新科技的人

eugenics /juˈdʒenɪks/ *n*.

the study of methods to improve the mental and physical characteristics of the human race by choosing who may become parents 优生学

dictate /ˈdɪkteɪt/ *v*.

to control or influence how sth. happens 支配；决定

equate /ɪˈkweɪt/ *v*.

to think that sth. is the same as sth. else or is as important 同等看待

wane /weɪn/ *v*.

to become gradually weaker or less important 减弱；衰败

Suggested Topics for Writing

1. In medical treatment, some people like a quick recovery undergoing a surgery while others prefer a slow but sure recovery using traditional medicine. What's your opinion? Use specific reasons and examples to support your answer.

2. Do you agree or disagree with the statement "People should be allowed to do any research which, they believe, would develop a new technology and eventually benefit the mankind"? Use specific reasons and examples to support your opinion.

（选文、注释：薛光荣）

Unit Eight   Coping Strategies

1. Water Damage

By Martha Southgate[1]

1   Cullen Jones and Lia Neal were among the many swimmers to win medals for the United States in this year's Olympic Games. ① But their inspiring performances obscure a disturbing truth. Not only are they, as African-Americans, anomalies in the elite levels of their sport, but enormous numbers of African-Americans do not have even rudimentary swimming skills, a lack that costs lives.

2   2010 study by the U.S.A. Swimming Foundation and the University of Memphis reported that nearly 70 percent of African-American children do not know how to swim. According to the Centers for Disease Control and Prevention, African-American children between the ages of 5 and 14 are almost three times more likely to drown than white children.

3   ② Cullen Jones could have been one of them; his parents put him in swim class after he almost drowned at the age of 5. Jones has become an evangelist for the importance of swimming lessons, working with Make a Splash, a water-safety initiative focused on minority children. But it can be tough even to give swimming lessons away. Starting last fall, the Boys and Girls Clubs of Boston made swimming lessons mandatory for their members, who are predominantly black and Hispanic. Though the lessons were free of charge, a number of

parents had to be talked into allowing their children to participate: they were terrified of letting them get in the water.

4   This bears out the U. S. A. Swimming Foundation's finding, in its 2010 report, that "fear trumped financial concerns across all respondent race groups in low-income families".

5   Regardless of race, the poor lack access to pools and swimming lessons. Around 40 percent of white children and 60 percent of Hispanic children do not know how to swim — they, too, could benefit from free or affordable lessons. But why is the problem worse among African-Americans, many of whom, across all economic classes, lack confidence in the water? A large part of that unease is a legacy of slavery and segregation.

6   ③ It has been documented that before slavery, many West Africans could and did swim. But a slave who could swim was a slave with another means of escape, so slave owners went to great lengths to make it impossible to keep this skill alive.

7   Later, segregation took its ugly toll at public beaches and pools. According to the historian Jeff Wiltse in an NPR[2] interview, "whites set up, essentially, sentinel guards at the entrance to the pool, and when black swimmers tried to come in and access them, they were beaten up, sometimes with clubs." One white motel manager was caught on camera pouring acid into a pool in which blacks were staging a "swim-in". Institutionalized racism was shored up by specious scholarship, like a 1969 report titled "The Negro and Learning to Swim: The Buoyancy Problem Related to Reported Biological Difference".

8   ④ Sadly, the fear of water that was instilled in African-Americans back then has become self-perpetuating. "Don't you know blacks don't swim?" Jones remembers being told by members of his family. It's time to bury that stereotype at sea. As of 2010, 15 European countries had made swimming a compulsory part of their education curriculums. Ideally, the United States would do the same. Not likely, I know, when even dry land physical education

programs are being slashed. But we can and should do better.

9   This country is blessed with a network of community centers like the Y.M.C.A. and the Boys and Girls Clubs that have swimming programs, instructors and pools in place. These centers could take Boston's example and make swimming lessons mandatory, which would benefit their clientele, regardless of its racial makeup. Public schools (and particularly charter schools, many of which have extended their school years into summer's heat) could devote part of each summer to shuttling their students to swim programs.

10   Another model is the public-private partnership, like Horizons National, an academic summer program that partners low-income schools with independent schools and colleges that have access to swimming pools. Here's a quote (posted on the program's Website) from one participant: "When I started Horizons I was so afraid of the water that I would not even go in the shallow end. Learning how to swim and overcoming that fear helped me realize that I could do anything." Who said this? Algernon Kelley, who now has a PhD in chemistry and lectured at Xavier University of Louisiana.

11   ⑤ The best way to eliminate the culture of anxiety around swimming is to create thousands of little African-American swimmers who are not afraid. I was one of those swimmers — never elite but always joyous. My parents packed me and my siblings off to the pool at our local community center as soon as we were old enough, and I became the kind of kid who would get out of the water only when my lips were blue. How wonderful if more children could feel the joy and confidence I feel when I'm swimming — and be safer around the water, too.

12   The United States faces immense problems of all kinds, many of which are more pressing than teaching children to swim. But for a mother who stands screaming on the shore as her child goes under for the last time, not knowing how to swim is the biggest problem there is.

(From *The New York Times*, August 10, 2012)

Notes

[1] **Martha Southgate**: The author of four novels. Her newest, *The Taste of Salt*, is available in bookstores and online now. Her previous novel, *Third Girl from the Left* won the Best Novel of the Year Award from the Black Caucus of the American Library Association and was shortlisted for the PEN/Beyond Margins Award and the Hurston/Wright Legacy Award. Her novel *The Fall of Rome* received the 2003 Alex Award from the American Library Association and was named one of the best novels of 2002 by Jonathan Yardley of *The Washington Post*. She is also the author of *Another Way to Dance*, which won the Coretta Scott King Genesis Award for Best First Novel. She received a 2002 New York Foundation for the Arts grant and has received fellowships from the MacDowell Colony, the Virginia Center for the Creative Arts and the Bread Loaf Writers Conference. Her July 2007 essay from *The New York Times Book Review*, "Writers Like Me" received considerable notice and appears in the anthology Best African-American Essays 2009. Previous non-fiction articles have appeared in *The New York Times Magazine*, *O*, *Premiere*, and *Essence*.

[2] **National Public Radio (NPR)**: A privately and publicly funded non-profit membership media organization that serves as a national syndicator to a network of 900 public radio stations in the United States.

Words and Phrases

obscure /əbˈskjuə(r)/ *v*.

to make it difficult to see, hear or understand 使模糊

anomaly /əˈnɒməli/ *n*.

a thing, situation, etc. that is different from what is normal or expected 异常事物

rudimentary /ˌruːdɪˈmentri/ *adj.*

dealing with only the most basic matters or ideas 基础的

mandatory /ˈmændətəri/ *adj.*

required by law 强制的

trump /trʌmp/ *v.*

to beat sth. that sb. says or does by saying or doing sth. even better 胜过

sentinel /ˈsentɪnl/ *n.*

a soldier whose job is to guard sth. 哨兵

swim-in /ˈswɪmɪn/ *n.*

an activity in segregated swimming pools for protest 游泳示威

institutionalized /ˌɪnstɪˈtjuːʃənəlaɪzd/ *adj.*

that has happened or been done for so long that it is considered normal 成惯例的

specious /ˈspiːʃəs/ *adj.*

seeming right or true but actually wrong or false 似是而非的

self-perpetuating /ˈselfpəˈpetʃueɪtɪŋ/ *adj.*

continuing without any outside influence 自我持续的

go to great lengths (to do sth.)

to put a lot of effort into doing sth., especially when this seems extreme 竭尽全力

shore up

to help to support sth. that is weak or going to fall 支撑

Reading Comprehension Questions

1. Which of the following is true about Cullen Jones? _____

   (A) He started to learn to swim before the age of 5.

   (B) He tries to enable minority children to learn to swim.

(C) His swimming skills are common among African-Americans.

(D) His success as a swimmer will make swimming lessons affordable.

2. According to the author, what is the main reason that so many African-Americans do not know how to swim? _____

   (A) Financial concerns.

   (B) A legacy of slavery and segregation.

   (C) A cut in physical education programs.

   (D) Lack of access to pools and swimming lessons.

3. We learn from the text that _____.

   (A) around 40 percent of white children do not know how to swim because of fear of water

   (B) African Americans have trouble learning to swim for biological reasons

   (C) slave owners tried hard to prevent black slaves from learning to swim

   (D) racism no longer has any effect on African-Americans

4. The phrase "to bury that stereotype at sea" in paragraph 8 most probably means _____.

   (A) to eliminate the false idea that blacks do not swim

   (B) to make swimming a compulsory part of education curriculums

   (C) to shuttle students to swim programs each summer

   (D) to remove the fear of water

5. We learn from the last three paragraphs that _____.

   (A) the author is an African-American

   (B) as a child, the author could not access a swimming pool

   (C) not knowing how to swim is the biggest problem in the United States

   (D) Algernon Kelley overcame his fear of water as a result of his academic achievement

(选文、注释:任爱军)

2. How to Write

By Colson Whitehead[1]

1 The art of writing can be reduced to a few simple rules. I share them with you now.

2 Rule No. 1: Show and Tell. ① <u>Most people say, "Show, don't tell," but I stand by Show and Tell, because when writers put their work out into the world, they're like kids bringing their broken unicorns and chewed-up teddy bears into class in the sad hope that someone else will love them as much as they do.</u> "And what do you have for us today, Marcy?" "A penetrating psychological study of a young med student who receives disturbing news from a former lover." "How marvelous! Timmy, what are you holding there?" "It's a Calvinoesque[2] romp through an unnamed metropolis much like New York, narrated by an armadillo." "Such imagination!" Show and Tell, followed by a good nap.

3 Rule No. 2: Don't go searching for a subject, let your subject find you. You can't rush inspiration. How do you think Capote[3] came to "In Cold Blood"? It was just an ordinary day when he picked up the paper to read his horoscope, and there it was — fate. Whether it's a harrowing account of a multiple homicide, a botched Everest expedition or a colorful family of singers trying to escape from Austria when the Nazis invade, you can't force it. ② <u>Once your subject finds you, it's like falling in love. It will be your constant companion. Shadowing you, peeping in your windows, calling you at all hours to leave messages like, "Only you understand me." Your ideal subject should be like a stalker with limitless resources, living off the inheritance he received after the suspiciously sudden death of his father.</u> He's in your apartment pawing your stuff when you're not around, using your toothbrush and cutting out all the

really good synonyms from the thesaurus. Don't be afraid: you have a best seller on your hands.

4 Rule No. 3: Write what you know. Bellow[4] once said, "Fiction is the higher autobiography." In other words, fiction is payback for those who have wronged you. When people read my books *My Gym Teacher Was an Abusive Bully* and *She Called Them Brussels Sprouts: A Survivor's Tale*, they're often surprised when I tell them they contain an autobiographical element. ③ <u>Therein lies the art, I say. How do you make that which is your everyday into the stuff of literature? Listen to your heart. Ask your heart, Is it true? And if it is, let it be. Once the lawyers sign off, you're good to go.</u>

5 Rule No. 4: Never use three words when one will do. Be concise. Don't fall in love with the gentle trilling of your mellifluous sentences. Learn how to "kill your darlings", as they say.

6 Rule No. 5: Keep a dream diary.

7 Rule No. 6: What isn't said is as important as what is said. In many classic short stories, the real action occurs in the silences. Try to keep all the good stuff off the page. Some "real world" practice might help. The next time your partner comes home, ignore his or her existence for 30 minutes, and then blurt out "That's it!" and drive the car onto the neighbor's lawn. When your children approach at bedtime, squeeze their shoulders meaningfully and, if you're a woman, smear your lipstick across your face with the back of your wrist, or, if you're a man, weep violently until they say, "It's OK, Dad." Drink out of a chipped mug, a souvenir from a family vacation or weekend getaway in better times, one that can trigger a two-paragraph compare/contrast description later on. It's a bit like Method acting[5]. Simply let this thought guide your every word and gesture: "Something is wrong — can you guess what it is?" If you're going for something a little more postmodern, repeat the above, but with fish.

8 Rule No. 7: Writer's block is a tool — use it. When asked why you haven't produced anything lately, just say, "I'm blocked." Since most people

think that writing is some mystical process where characters "talk to you" and you can hear their voices in your head, being blocked is the perfect cover for when you just don't feel like working. The gods of creativity bless you, they forsake you, it's out of your hands and whatnot. Writer's block is like "We couldn't get a baby sitter" or "I ate some bad shrimp", an excuse that always gets you a pass. ④ <u>The electric company nagging you for money, your cell provider harassing you, whatever — just say, "I'm blocked", and you're off the hook. But don't overdo it. In the same way the baby-sitter bit loses credibility when your kids are in grad school, there's an expiration date. After 20 years, you might want to mix it up. Throw in an Ellisonian[6] "My house caught fire and burned up my opus." The specifics don't matter — the important thing is to figure out what works for you.</u>

9   Rule No. 8: Is secret.

10   Rule No. 9: Have adventures. ⑤ <u>The Hemingway mode was in ascendancy for decades before it was eclipsed by trendy fabulist "exercises". The pendulum is swinging back, though, and it's going to knock these effete eggheads right out of their Aeron chairs. Keep ahead of the curve. Get out and see the world.</u> It's not going to kill you to butch it up a tad. Book passage on a tramp steamer. Rustle up some dysentery; it's worth it for the fever dreams alone. Lose a kidney in a knife fight. You'll be glad you did.

11   Rule No. 10: Revise, revise, revise. I cannot stress this enough. Revision is when you do what you should have done the first time, but didn't. It's like washing the dishes two days later instead of right after you finish eating. Get that draft counter going. Remove a comma and then print out another copy — that's another draft right there. Do this enough times and you can really get those numbers up, which will come in handy if someone challenges you to a draft-off. When the ref blows the whistle and your opponent goes, "26 drafts!", you'll bust out with "216!" and send them to the mat.

12   Rule No. 11: There are no rules. If everyone jumped off a bridge, would you do it, too? No. There are no rules except the ones you learned during your

Show and Tell days. Have fun. If they don't want to be friends with you, they're not worth being friends with. Most of all, just be yourself.

(From *The New York Times*, July 26, 2012.)

Notes

[1] **Colson Whitehead**(1969 –   ): A New York-based novelist, he is the author of six novels, including his debut work, the 1999 novel *The Intuitionist*, and the National Book Award-winning novel *The Underground Railroad*. He has also published two books of non-fiction. In 2002, he received a MacArthur Fellowship.

[2] **Calvinoesque**: In the style of Calvino. Italo Calvino (1923 – 1985) was an Italian journalist and writer of short stories and novels. His best known works include *Our Ancestors* (1952 – 1959), *Cosmicomics* (1965), *Invisible Cities* (1972) and *If on a Winter's Night a Traveler* (1979). He started as a political neorealist, and later moved away from realism, first toward modernism and fantasy, eventually toward full maturation as a postmodern writer.

[3] **Capote**: Truman Garcia Capote (1924 – 1984) was an American novelist, screenwriter, playwright, and actor, many of whose short stories, novels, plays, and nonfiction are recognized literary classics, including the novella *Breakfast at Tiffany's* (1958) and the true crime novel *In Cold Blood* (1966), which he labeled a "nonfiction novel". At least 20 films and television dramas have been produced of Capote novels, stories, and plays.

[4] **Bellow**: Saul Bellow (1915 – 2005) was a Canadian-American writer. For his literary work, Bellow was awarded the Pulitzer Prize, the Nobel Prize for Literature, and the National Medal of Arts. He is the only writer to win the National Book Award for Fiction three times and he received the National Book Foundation's Lifetime Medal for Distinguished Contribution to American

Letters in 1990.

[5] **Method Acting**: Preparation for an acting role in which the actor gets real experience of the life of the type of character that he or she will play. Specifically, it refers to a range of training and rehearsal techniques that seek to encourage sincere and emotionally expressive performances, as formulated by a number of different theatre practitioners, principally in the United States, where it is among the most popular—and controversial—approaches to acting. These techniques built on the Stanislavski's "system" of the Russian actor and director Konstantin Stanislavski.

[6] **Ellisonian**: In the way that is typical of Ellison's writing. Ralph Waldo Ellison (1913 – 1994) was an American novelist, literary critic, and scholar. He was born in Oklahoma City, Oklahoma. Ellison is best known for his novel *Invisible Man*, which won the National Book Award in 1953. He also wrote *Shadow and Act* (1964), a collection of political, social and critical essays, and *Going to the Territory* (1986). For *The New York Times*, the best of these essays in addition to the novel put him "among the gods of America's literary Parnassus". A posthumous novel, *Juneteenth*, was published after being assembled from voluminous notes he left after his death.

Words and Phrases

romp /rɔmp/ *n.*

　one, especially a girl, who behaves in a boyish manner　顽皮的女孩；顽皮嬉闹

armadillo /ˌɑːməˈdɪləʊ/ *n.*

　a small wild animal from hot parts of North and South America whose body is covered with pieces of a hard substance forming a shell　犰狳

horoscope /ˈhɒrəskəʊp/ *n.*

　a description of someone's character and the likely events in their life that is based on astrology the position of the stars and the date they were born　星座

运势

harrowing /ˈhærəʊɪŋ/ n.

extremely worrying, upsetting, or frightening 令人痛苦的

homicide /ˈhɒmɪsaɪd/ n.

the act or an instance of unlawfully killing another human being 过失杀人

botch /bɒtʃ/ v.

to do something very badly out of clumsiness or lack of care 弄糟

peep /piːp/ v.

to look quickly or secretly 偷看

stalker /ˈstɔːkə(r)/ n.

someone who hunts a person or animal by following them without being seen 跟踪者

paw /pɔː/ v.

to touch somebody or something, or caress somebody, roughly or rudely with the hands 乱摸

thesaurus /θɪˈsɔːrəs/ n.

a book that lists words related to each other in meaning, usually giving synonyms and antonyms 词库

bully /ˈbʊli/ n.

an aggressive person who intimidates or mistreats weaker people 欺凌者

sprout /spraʊt/ n.

a new growth on a plant 新芽

trill /trɪl/ v.

to play, sing, pronounce, or utter something with a high-pitched warbling sound 啼啭

mellifluous /meˈlɪfluəs/ adj.

pleasant and soothing to listen to, and sweet or rich in tone 悦耳动听的

souvenir /ˌsuːvəˈnɪə(r)/ n.

something that you buy on vacation or at a special event to remind you later of being there 纪念品

getaway /ˈgeɪtweɪ/ *n.*

a short vacation or break 短假

forsake /fəˈseɪk/ *v.*

(forsook, forsaken) to give up, renounce, or sacrifice something that gives pleasure 抛弃；摒弃

whatnot /ˈwɒtnɒt/ *n.*

something of the same or a similar kind 诸如此类的东西

nag /næg/ *v.*

to find fault with somebody regularly and repeatedly 唠叨

harass /ˈhærəs/ *v.*

to persistently annoy, attack, or bother somebody 骚扰

opus /ˈəʊpəs/ *n.*

an important piece of work by a writer, artist, etc. 大作

ascendancy /əˈsendənsi/ *n.*

a position of power or domination over others 优势

trendy /ˈtrendi/ *adj.*

extremely fashionable, but often silly or annoying 时髦的；赶时髦的

fabulist /ˈfæbjʊlɪst/ *n.*

somebody who composes or recites fables 寓言作家

effete /ɪˈfiːt/ *adj.*

lacking or having lost the strength or ability to get things done 衰弱的

egghead /ˈeghed/ *n.*

an intellectual or bookish person 书呆子

dysentery /ˈdɪsəntri/ *n.*

inflammation of the bowels, causing severe diarrhoea, usual with a discharge of mucus and blood 痢疾

ref /ref/ *n.*

(informal) = referee, somebody whose job is to make sure that players in a game obey the rules 裁判

live off

to depend on somebody or something as a source of financial support or for a livelihood 靠……生活

cutting out

remove part from text 从……中挑出

sign off

to give approval to something 同意

blurt out

to say something suddenly or impulsively 脱口而出

off the hook

(informal) free of a difficult situation 摆脱困境;脱身

butch it up

to become extremely masculine and strong 有男人气派

a tad

a little bit 一点点

rustle up

to quickly find and bring together things or people 筹措

Suggested Topics for Writing

1. Someone thinks that science students don't need to learn the art of writing at all. Someone thinks otherwise. What is your opinion about the issue? Use specific details or examples to prove your view.

2. American writer Gene Fowler said: "The best way to become a successful writer is to read good writing, remember it, and then forget where you remember it from." Do you agree or disagree with his statement? Use specific reasons and examples to support your answer.

(选文、注释:徐守平)

Unit Nine Surviving Skills

1. Survival of the Biggest
Editorial by *Economist*[1]

Concern about the clout of the internet giants is growing. But antitrust watchdogs should tread carefully.

1   The four giants of the internet age — Google, Apple, Facebook and Amazon — are extraordinary creatures. Never before has the world seen firms grow so fast or spread their tentacles so widely. Apple has become a colossus of capitalism, accounting for 4.3% of the value of the Standard and Poor 500[2] and 1.1% of the global equity market. Some 425m(million) people now use its iTunes online store, whose virtual shelves are packed with music and other digital content. Google, meanwhile, is the undisputed global leader in search and online advertising. ① <u>Its Android software powers three-quarters of the smartphones being shipped. Amazon dominates the online-retail and e-book markets in many countries; less well known is its behind-the-scenes power in cloud computing. As for Facebook, if the social network's one billion users were a country, it would be the world's third largest.</u>

2   The digital revolution these giants have helped foment has brought huge benefits to consumers and businesses, and promoted free speech and the spread of democracy along the way. Yet they provoke fear as well as wonder. Their size and speed can, if left unchecked, be used to choke off competition. That is

why they are attracting close scrutiny from regulators.

3   ② Google is the one most under threat. Both the European Commission and America's Federal Trade Commission (FTC) have been investigating allegations that it has unfairly manipulated its search results to favour its own services. The company also stands accused of several other transgressions, including using patents to hinder competition in the smartphone market. The regulators want Google, which disputes the charges, to change its practices. If talks fail — they were still continuing as *The Economist* went to press — the search firm could end up mired in costly legal fights on both sides of the Atlantic. This could become the defining antitrust battle of the internet age, just as Microsoft's epic fight a decade ago — over its bundling of its web-browser with its Windows operating system — defined the personal-computer era.

Why Size Matters

4   Three trends alarm those who think the digital giants are becoming too powerful for consumers' good. The first is the rise of winner-take-almost-all markets on the internet. Although Microsoft has poured money into its rival search engine, Bing, Google still accounts for over two-thirds of searches undertaken in America and a whopping 90% or so of them in some European markets. Facebook, too, enjoys a quasi-monopoly in the social-networking arena. Rivals fear that the big four will exploit their dominant status in their main businesses to gain an unfair advantage in other areas — a charge that lies at the heart of the antitrust case against Google.

5   Second, the giants want to get consumers hooked on their own "platforms" — combinations of online services and apps that run on smartphones and tablet computers. ③ These platforms can be very appealing. Apple mints money because its hugely profitable iPhone has, in effect, become a remote control for many people's digital lives. But there are worries that Apple and its peers are creating "walled gardens[3]" which make it hard for users to move content from one platform to another.

6 　The third concern is the internet giants' habit of gobbling up promising firms before they become a threat. Amazon, which raised $3 billion in a rare bond issue this week, has splashed out on firms such as Zappos, an online shoe retailer that had ambitions to rival it. Facebook and Google have made big acquisitions too, such as Instagram and AdMob, some of which have drawn intense scrutiny from regulators.

7 　So far the watchdogs have focused on surgical strikes, in areas such as online search and the e-book market (where Apple is under investigation for alleged cartel-like behaviour with several publishers). Their goal has been to get swift settlements with negotiated remedies that curtail bad behaviour.

8 　Some critics think that is too weak. There have been calls for Google to be chopped up into two independent firms, severing its search business from its other activities. ④ <u>Tim Wu, a professor at Columbia Law School and consultant to the FTC, has even argued that in the interests of promoting competition, big "information monopolies" such as Apple and Google should be forced to choose between being providers of digital content, producers of hardware or information distributors (via such things as cloud-computing services).</u>

9 　The danger is that such corporate butchery would do more harm than good. The fact that people have flocked to big web firms' platforms suggests that consumers are perfectly willing to trade some openness for convenience and ease-of-use. And if they do want to change providers, the cost of doing so has fallen dramatically in the broadband era. Switching to a new search engine or music service takes a matter of seconds. And this time, rather than being one dominant player (as Microsoft was for a while), there is a war of all against all.

10 　⑤ <u>Smartphones powered by Google's Android operating system have come from nowhere to dominate the market, eclipsing Apple's iPhone. Amazon's Kindle tablet is going head-to-head with the iPad. In social networking Google+ is fighting Facebook. And Facebook and Apple, along with Microsoft, now have designs on Google's dominance in search.</u> Smaller firms such as Twitter are also keen to join the giants' ranks, and have rebuffed marriage offers from them.

Facebook itself was a start-up just eight years ago.

(From *Economist*, December 1, 2012)

Notes

[1] *Economist*: Weekly magazine of news and opinions, generally regarded as one of the world's preeminent journals of its kind. It gives thorough and wide-ranging coverage of general news and particularly of international political developments that bear on the world's economy.

[2] **The Standard and Poor 500**: The S & P 500, is an American stock market index based on the market capitalization of 500 large companies having common stock listed on the NYSE or NASDAQ. The S & P 500 index components and their weightings are determined by S & P Dow Jones Indices. It is one of the most commonly followed equity indices, and many consider it one of the best representations of the U.S. stock market, and a bellwether for the U.S. economy.

[3] **Walled Garden**: A closed platform, walled garden or closed ecosystem is a software system where the carrier or service provider has control over applications, content, and media, and restricts convenient access to non-approved applications or content. This is in contrast to an open platform, where consumers have unrestricted access to applications, content, and much more.

Words and Phrases

clout /klaʊt/ n.
power or the authority to influence other people's decisions 影响力；势力

antitrust /ˌæntɪˈtrʌst/ adj.
intended to prevent companies from unfairly controlling prices 反托拉斯的；反垄断的

foment /fəʊˈment/ v.

stir up, cause trouble 激起；煽动（麻烦等）

scrutiny /ˈskruːtɪnɪ/ *n.*

careful and thorough examination of sb. or sth. 仔细的观察；监督

allegation /ˌæləˈgeɪʃən/ *n.*

a statement that sb. has done sth. wrong or illegal, but that has not been proved 指控；陈述；主张；宣称

transgression /trænzˈgreʃn/ *n.*

to do sth. that is against the rules of social behaviour or against a moral principle 违反；违法

bundle /ˈbʌndl/ *v.*

to include computer software or other services with a new computer at no extra cost （尤指出售计算机时）赠送软件

monopoly /məˈnɒpəli/ *n.*

large company that controls all or most of a business activity 垄断；专卖；垄断者

acquisition /ˌækwɪˈzɪʃən/ *n.*

the act of getting land, power, money 收购

curtail /kɜːˈteɪl/ *v.*

to reduce or limit something 缩短；剥夺

eclipse /ɪˈklɪps/ *v.*

to become more important, powerful, famous etc. than sb. or sth. else, so that they are no longer noticed 使黯然失色；形成日食或月食

rebuff /rɪˈbʌf/ *v.*

reject outright and bluntly 断然拒绝；阻碍

account for

to form a particular amount or part of something 在数量、比例上占

gobble up

to eat something very quickly, especially in an impolite or greedy way; if one company gobbles up a smaller company, it buys it and takes control of it 吞噬；吞并

in the interests of

in order to make a situation or system fair, safe　为……利益起见

Reading Comprehension Questions

1. According to the author, the giants of the internet age are causing so much fear that _____.
   (A) they are promoting free speech
   (B) democracy is being spread all the way
   (C) competition is being reduced
   (D) government officials are making careful inspections

2. Google's trouble may lie in that _____.
   (A) it is manipulating its search results
   (B) *The Economist* went to press
   (C) it may face many lawsuits in both Europe and America
   (D) it can define the personal-computer era

3. By "winner-take-almost-all markets" the author means to refer to the kind of markets in which _____.
   (A) the winner of one field will use its influence to win in other fields
   (B) the winner of one business will take away all the profits
   (C) the dominant status of the winner in the main businesses will be enhanced
   (D) a charge that lies at the heart of the antitrust case will happen to the winner

4. What is the countermeasure that the regulators use to relieve people of their concerns? _____
   (A) Making surgeries.　　(B) Preventing inquisitions.
   (C) Quick strikes.　　　 (D) Intense scrutinies.

5. The fact that people have flocked to big web firms' platforms suggests that consumers prefer _____.
   (A) convenience　　　　(B) some kind of corporate butchery
   (C) openness　　　　　 (D) switching to new services

(选文:徐守平;注释:管琛)

2. How Reading Good Works Makes Us More Effective?

By Kirpal Singh[1]

1 I am a writer. I am also a teacher. Being both, I am frequently asked how and in what ways Literature makes us better. How does it help us achieve better results in our home, workplace and community? What are the practical uses of reading a book?

2 Let me begin with Shakespeare. In *Macbeth*[2], we hear Duncan, the King of Scotland, make this observation:

There's no art.

To find the mind's construction in the face:

He was a gentleman on whom I built.

An absolute trust.

3 ① <u>These lines strike a most familiar chord, for they draw our attention to the fact that appearances can be — and very frequently are — deceiving. How often have we repeated these very same sentiments in our lives? "I thought he was a good person." Or, "Looking at him I never would have thought he'd do such a thing!"</u>

4 Duncan's words reflect one of the greatest lessons of life and living. If we heed the meaning of these words, we discover much about our world and ourselves. And we'll move forward, knowing how easily we can be duped and how we have to be ever vigilant.

5 Mahatma Gandhi[3] wrote:

Because I am their leader I must follow them.

6 All of us know about leaders; some of us are leaders ourselves, others report to leaders or follow them. ② <u>At one point or other, in some context, I

think we are all called upon to display leadership skills. Gandhi states the most essential skill a good leader must possess and show is humility. Humility personified through example. This is a rare quality, which few great leaders in history have demonstrated — the capacity to follow the people they lead.

7   I'd like to highlight another critical practical use of literature: its ability to help us become better communicators. We live in an age given to everything instant. The world of social media (Facebook, Twitter) demands that we say what we want to say fast, quickly, briefly, and right now! And yet our human experience tells us that in doing this we sacrifice Truth because it's hard to say what we experience quickly and briefly. Here is where Literature comes into play.

8   ③ Literature provides a kind of shorthand for the transmission of feelings and thoughts. For example, when asked to define the term Literature itself, a tenth century general said:

9   *Literature is heaven and hell trapped in a cage.*

10   If you imagine for a moment, just how rich these words are, you will realise how we constantly borrow this phrase in response to difficult questions ... "you know, I'm really trapped, my life seems to be both heaven and hell, but, like, trapped in a cage!"

11   ④ Through literature, we not only learn how to read both between and beyond the lines, we also learn how to convey meanings better. And this is because the best literary writing is always metaphoric — a vast storehouse of human experience! Literature is our linguistic heritage and a powerful resource which our schools and universities don't give enough credence to.

12   Let me end as I began, with a few lines from the great writer/poet William Blake:

   I was angry with my friend:
   I told my wrath, my wrath did end.
   I was angry with my foe;
   I told it not, my wrath did grow.

13 These lines are forceful in their simplicity and lyricism. They come from a poem entitled *A Poison Tree*. ⑤ <u>As our lives grow richer or poorer, depending on the quality of our many relationships, so the wisdom contained in these lines will help us chart and deepen our sense of how to manage said relationships. I challenge you to read Blake's poem. Understand its meaning, and you'll be changed.</u>

(From Reader's Digest. November, 2011. https://www.smu.edu.sg/sites/default/files/smu/news_room/smu_in_the_news/2011/sources/RD_201111_1.pdf)

Notes

[1] **Kirpal Singh** (1894 – 1974): A spiritual master. He was the President of the "World Fellowship of Religions", an organization recognized by UNESCO (United Nations Educational, Scientific, and Cultural Organization), which had representatives from all the main religions of the world.

[2] ***Macbeth***: Shakespeare's shortest tragedy, and tells the story of a brave Scottish general named Macbeth who receives a prophecy from a trio of witches that one day he will become King of Scotland. Consumed by ambition and spurred to action by his wife, Macbeth murders King Duncan and takes the throne for himself. He is then wracked with guilt and paranoia, and he soon becomes a tyrannical ruler as he is forced to commit more and more murders to protect himself from enmity and suspicion. The bloodbath and consequent civil war swiftly take Macbeth and Lady Macbeth into the realms of arrogance, madness, and death.

[3] **Mohandas Gandhi** (1869 – 1948): Preeminent leader of Indian nationalism and prophet of nonviolence in the 20th century. Gandhi won the affection and loyalty of millions and became known as the Mahatma ("Great-souled").

Words and Phrases

vigilant /ˈvɪdʒɪlənt/ *adj.*

carefully observant or attentive; on the lookout for possible danger 警觉的；机警的

humility /hjuˈmɪləti/ *n.*

a disposition to be humble; a lack of false pride 谦逊；谦恭

personify /pəˈsɒnɪfaɪ/ *v.*

to have a lot of particular qualities or be a typical example of something 人格化；体现

metaphorical /ˌmetəˈfɒrɪkl/ *adj.*

expressing one thing in terms normally denoting another 隐喻性的

give credence to sth.

to believe or accept sth. as true 相信；信任

Suggested Topics for Writing

1. Do you think literature can make us better? Use specific reasons and examples to support your answer.

2. "Literature provides a kind of shorthand for the transmission of feelings and thoughts." Do you agree or disagree with the quotation above? Use specific reasons and examples to explain your position.

(选文:任爱军;注释:管琛)

Unit Ten Education Issues

1. The Trouble with Online Education

By Mark Edmundson[1]

1 "Ah, you're a professor. You must learn so much from your students."

2 This line, which I've heard in various forms, always makes me cringe. Do people think that lawyers learn a lot about the law from their clients? That patients teach doctors much of what they know about medicine?

3 Yet latent in the sentiment that our students are our teachers is an important truth. We do in fact need to learn from them, but not about the history of the Roman Empire or the politics of "*Paradise Lost*[2]". Understanding what it is that students have to teach teachers can help us to deal with one of the most vexing issues now facing colleges and universities: online education. At my school, the University of Virginia, that issue did more than vex us; it came close to tearing the university apart.

4 A few weeks ago our president, Teresa A. Sullivan, was summarily dismissed and then summarily reinstated by the university's board of visitors[3]. One reason for her dismissal was the perception that she was not moving forward fast enough on Internet learning. Stanford was doing it, Harvard, Yale and M.I.T. too. But Virginia, it seemed, was lagging. Just this week, in fact, it was announced that Virginia, along with a number of other universities, signed on with a company called Coursera to develop and offer online classes.

5   But can online education ever be education of the very best sort?

6   It's here that the notion of students teaching teachers is illuminating. As a friend and fellow professor said to me: "You don't just teach students, you have to learn from them too." It took a minute — it sounded like he was channeling Huck Finn[4] — but I figured it out.

7   ① <u>With every class we teach, we need to learn who the people in front of us are. We need to know where they are intellectually, who they are as people and what we can do to help them grow. Teaching, even when you have a group of a hundred students on hand, is a matter of dialogue.</u>

8   In the summer Shakespeare course I'm teaching now, I'm constantly working to figure out what my students are able to do and how they can develop. Can they grasp the contours of Shakespeare's plots? If not, it's worth adding a well-made film version of the next play to the syllabus. Is the language hard for them, line to line? Then we have to spend more time going over individual speeches word by word. Are they adept at understanding the plot and the language? Time to introduce them to the complexities of Shakespeare's rendering of character.

9   ② <u>Every memorable class is a bit like a jazz composition. There is the basic melody that you work with. It is defined by the syllabus. But there is also a considerable measure of improvisation against that disciplining background.</u>

10 Something similar applies even to larger courses. We tend to think that the spellbinding lecturers we had in college survey classes were gifted actors who could strut and fret[5] 50 amazing minutes on the stage. But I think that the best of those lecturers are highly adept at reading their audiences. They use practical means to do this — tests and quizzes, papers and evaluations. But they also deploy something tantamount to artistry. They are superb at sensing the mood of a room. They have a sort of pedagogical sixth sense. They feel it when the class is engaged and when it slips off. And they do something about it. Their every joke is a sounding. It's a way of discerning who is out there on a

given day.

11   ③ A large lecture class can also create genuine intellectual community. Students will always be running across others who are also enrolled, and they'll break the ice with a chat about it and maybe they'll go on from there. When a teacher hears a student say, "My friends and I are always arguing about your class," he knows he's doing something right. From there he folds what he has learned into his teaching, adjusting his course in a fluid and immediate way that the Internet professor cannot easily match.

12   Online education is a one-size-fits-all endeavor. It tends to be a monologue and not a real dialogue. The Internet teacher, even one who responds to students via e-mail, can never have the immediacy of contact that the teacher on the scene can, with his sensitivity to unspoken moods and enthusiasms. This is particularly true of online courses for which the lectures are already filmed and in the can. It doesn't matter who is sitting out there on the Internet watching; the course is what it is.

13   Not long ago I watched a pre-filmed online course from Yale about the New Testament[6]. It was a very good course. ④ The instructor was hyper-intelligent, learned and splendidly articulate. But the course wasn't great and could never have been. There were Yale students on hand for the filming, but the class seemed addressed to no one in particular. It had an anonymous quality. In fact there was nothing you could get from that course that you couldn't get from a good book on the subject.

14   A truly memorable college class, even a large one, is a collaboration between teacher and students. It's a one-time-only event. Learning at its best is a collective enterprise, something we've known since Socrates[7]. ⑤ You can get knowledge from an Internet course if you're highly motivated to learn. But in real courses the students and teachers come together and create an immediate and vital community of learning. A real course creates intellectual joy, at least in some. I don't think an Internet course ever will. Internet learning promises

to make intellectual life more sterile and abstract than it already is — and also, for teachers and for students alike, far more lonely.

(From *The New York Times*, July 20, 2012)

Notes

[1] **Mark Edmundson**: University professor, specialties, poet, romanticism, written some books, such as *Self and Soul: A Defense of Ideals* (2015); *Why Football Matters; My Education in the Game* (2014); *Why Teach?* (2013); *The Fine Wisdom and Perfect Teachings of the Kings of Rock and Roll* (2010); *The Death of Sigmund Freud* (2008).

[2] *Paradise Lost*: An epic poem written by the 17th-century English poet John Milton (1608—1674). It is considered to be Milton's major work, and it helped solidify his reputation as one of the greatest English poets of his time. The poem concerns the Biblical story of the Fall of Man: the temptation of Adam and Eve by the fallen angel Satan and their expulsion from the Garden of Eden. Milton's purpose is to "justify the ways of God to men".

[3] **Board of Visitors**: A body of elected or appointed members who jointly oversee the activities of a company or organization. Other names include board of governors, board of managers, board of regents, board of trustees, and board of directors. It is often simply referred to as "the board".

[4] **Huck Finn**: A fictional character created by Mark Twain. Huck Finn is the son of the town's vagrant drunkard. Huck lives the life of a destitute vagabond. Due to his unconventional childhood, Huck has received almost no education. The author metaphorically names him "the juvenile pariah of the village" and describes Huck as "idle, and lawless, and vulgar, and bad" qualities.

[5] **Strut and Fret**: Strut and fret takes its title from a line in William Shakespeare's Macbeth, from Macbeth's famous soliloquy: "Out, out, brief

candle! Life's but a walking shadow, a poor player that struts and frets his hour upon the stage and then is heard no more: it is a tale told by an idiot, full of sound and fury, signifying nothing."

[6] *New Testament*: The New Testament is the second major part of the Christian biblical canon, the first part being the *Old Testament*, which is based on the *Hebrew Bible*. The *New Testament* discusses the teachings of Jesus, called "gospels", as well as events in first-century Christianity. Christians regard both the Old and New Testaments together as sacred scripture. The *New Testament* has influenced religious, philosophical, and political movements in Christendom, and left an indelible mark on literature, art, and music.

[7] **Socrates**: A classical Greek (Athenian) philosopher credited as one of the founders of Western philosophy. His most important contribution to Western method of inquiry, known as the Socratic method, which he largely applied to the examination of key moral concepts such as the Good and Justice.

Words and Phrases

cringe /krɪndʒ/ v.
to feel very embarrassed and uncomfortable about something 畏缩

latent /ˈleɪtnt/ adj.
existing, but not yet very noticeable, active or well developed 潜在的；休眠的

vex /veks/ v.
to annoy or worry somebody 使烦恼；使苦恼

reinstate /ˌriːɪnˈsteɪt/ v.
to give back a job or position that had been taken away from somebody 使复原；使恢复

illuminate /ɪˈluːmɪneɪt/ v.
to make something clearer or easier to understand 阐明；说明

channel /ˈtʃænl/ v.

to behave in the manner of somebody else, as though that person has given you the idea or desire to act in that way 引导;开导

contour /ˈkɒntʊə(r)/ n.

the outer edges of something; the outline of its shape or form 概要;轮廓

syllabus /ˈsɪləbəs/ n.

a list of the topics, books, etc. that students should study in a particular subject at school or college 教学大纲

improvisation /ˌɪmprəvaɪˈzeɪʃən/ n.

the act of inventing music, the words in a play, a statement, etc. while you are playing or speaking, instead of planning it in advance 即兴创作

discipline /ˈdɪsəplɪn/ v.

to control the way you behave and make yourself do things that you believe you should do 训练以使举止符合行为准则

spellbind /ˈspelbaɪnd/ v.

(past and past participle spellbound) Hold the complete attention of (someone) as though by magic 用符咒迷惑;迷住

deploy /dɪˈplɔɪ/ v.

to use something effectively 施展;有效地利用

tantamount /ˈtæntəˌmaʊnt/ adj.

having the same bad effect as something else 相等的;相当的

artistry /ˈɑːtɪstri/ n.

the skill of an artist 技艺;艺术性

pedagogical /ˌpedəˈgɒdʒɪkl/ adj.

relating to teaching 适宜于教师的,教学(法)的

sounding /ˈsaʊndɪŋ/ n.

a measurement that is made to find out how deep water is 探测仪;探测术

articulate /ɑːˈtɪkjuleɪt/ adj.

(of a person) good at expressing ideas or feelings clearly in words 善于表达的

motivate /ˈməʊtɪveɪt/ v.

to make somebody want to do something, especially something that involves hard work and effort 促动;激发

sterile /ˈsteraɪl/ *adj.*

lacking individual personality, imagination or new ideas 毫无新意的;乏味的

sign on

to sign a form or contract which says that you agree to do a job or become a soldier 签约受雇

figure out

to think about somebody/ something until you understand them/it 弄明白

Reading Comprehension Questions

1. According to the passage, the reason for T. A. Sullivan's being dismissed is that she was _____.

    (A) unable to handle her position properly

    (B) nominated as the university's board of visitors

    (C) considered slow on Internet learning

    (D) not collaborative with other universities like Yale and M.I.T.

2. What does the author have in mind when he says teaching is "a matter of dialogue"? _____

    (A) He needs students to inspire and acknowledge his lecture.

    (B) He needs to talk with students directly to put his ideas across.

    (C) He needs to express his ideas publicly as an actor with audience around.

    (D) He needs to know students' understanding and development by their direct feedback in class.

3. The author opposes on-line education for the following reasons except that it _____.

    (A) makes the lecturer feel dull and uncertain

    (B) loses instant contact with students on-line

(C) makes the lecturer unable to feel the mood and enthusiasm in class

(D) does not apply to any individual, but fits all

4. From the whole passage, we may find that the phrase "anonymous quality" in the last paragraph probably means _____.

   (A) the lecturer does not give his or her name

   (B) the students can get the course freely

   (C) the course is given to no one in particular

   (D) the subject of the course can be downloaded anywhere

5. The value of a good class in the author's mind is _____.

   (A) good academic environment created by universities as a whole

   (B) the humor that students enjoy

   (C) teachers' high teaching quality and enthusiasm

   (D) collaborative efforts between teachers and students

(选文、注释:丁菲菲)

2. Really Useful Schooling

By Adrian Tan[1]

The function of education is to prepare us for life. Here is what Adrian Tan thinks our schools should teach.

1　Life is complicated. It starts before we're ready, it continues while we're still trying to figure out the point of it. And it ends long before we've worked out just what to do. It's vital then that young people prepare for that journey as soon as they can. We're lucky because there is a brief, special time in their lives when they are meant to do just that — school.

2　① <u>For a few short years, our children are our captive audience. We are able to impart whatever knowledge we think will benefit them at some point of their lives. This is where the school system fails us. Because we try to make schools do a lot of other things at the same time.</u>

3　We want schools to act as cheap childcare centres, to keep our children occupied while the adults are occupied. So, we start school days early and stretch them throughout the day, even when we don't really need to. We also think our schools should separate clever kids from average kids. ② <u>So we teach them fiendishly complicated subjects like calculus and chemistry in order to see which kids are 2.3 percent better than their peers at those subjects. Apart from mathematicians and chemists, very few of us have any use for those subjects in the years ahead.</u>

4　If we agree that the function of education is to prepare us for life, then there is very little time to waste. We know that before long, our children will become bored, disillusioned, and far too large to intimidate. So, while we can, we ought to concentrate on teaching them really useful things. Here is what I think our schools should teach.

5   Courtesy — The sooner our young people learn this, the better. Politeness and consideration are the hallmarks of civilisation. In any case, a lot more can be accomplished by a smile and good manners than with a PhD.

6   Managing Money — Like it or not, for most of us, our adult lives will be consumed by the struggle for this. ③ It baffles me that we don't make an effort to teach our young people the rudiments of managing it. Is borrowing on a credit card a good thing? Should you take a second mortgage[2] if you have no income? How do you live within your means? No one should be expected to pick this up after leaving school (or worse, after getting a job). We have a responsibility to teach our young people this basic skill from the outset.

7   Critical thinking — Today, we're swamped by fact and opinion. There's always a temptation to accept something we are told, especially if it's well-crafted, especially if it's something we agree with. But that's not what educated people do. Educated people are rational and reasonable. They look at facts and they apply logic. If our schools teach nothing else, they should at least teach critical thinking.

8   Health — Kids should learn to take care of their bodies. They should know that if they eat junk, they will become fat and unhealthy. They should be very clear about what happens to their bodies when they drink, or smoke, or take drugs. They should know how people become pregnant. That's crucial when they enter puberty, and beyond. They really shouldn't have to learn about sex from the latest rap video.

9   Society — The idea here is that all of us are part of something much bigger. ④ We have rights and responsibilities. We ought to understand what they are, and why they are that way. We have to know a little bit of our immediate history and geography, because we need to have a context in which to relate to the people around us.

10   How will we test students on these subjects? We can't. How then will we

know they are learning? We won't. At least not immediately. But that's not a reason to avoid teaching important topics. We don't close down churches, mosques and temples just because we're not sure that the congregation is paying attention. We keep at it, because we can't afford not to.

11 Are these subjects too "low-brow"? Perhaps. Don't get me wrong: science and literature are important. There will always be a place in the world for quantum physicists and Shakespearean scholars. ⑤ But our schools cannot be designed to enable the best and the brightest to excel. They must also equip the weakest among us to survive. I can't think of a more noble purpose for our schools than for them to spend every moment they have telling this to our kids: "This is life, this is what you are going to face, and this is how you deal with it." Everything else is superfluity.

(From *Reader's Digest*, ASIA, November, 2010)

Notes

[1] **Adrian Tan:** Born in 1966, is a lawyer and author from Singapore. He is best known as the writer of the fiction novels *The Teenage Textbook* (1988) and *The Teenage Workbook* (1989), which were bestsellers in Singapore in the late-1980s.

[2] **A Second Mortgage:** A lien on a property which is subordinate to a more senior mortgage or loan. Called lien holders positioning the second mortgage falls behind the first mortgage. This means second mortgages are riskier for lenders and thus generally come with a higher interest rate than first mortgages. This is because if the loan goes into default, the first mortgage gets paid off first before the second mortgage. Commercial loans can have multiple loans as long as the equity supports it.

Words and Phrases

impart /ɪmˈpɑːt/ v.

to give information, knowledge, wisdom, etc. to sb. 传授

fiendishly /ˈfiːndɪʃli/ adv.

extremely difficult or complicated 凶猛地；刁钻地

intimidate /ɪnˈtɪmɪdeɪt/ v.

to frighten or threaten sb. into making them do what you want 恐吓；威胁

rudiments /ˈruːdɪmənts/ n.

the most basic parts of a subject, which you learn first (= basics) 初步；入门

puberty /ˈpjuːbətɪ/ n.

the stage in someone's life when their body starts to become physically mature 青春期

congregation /ˌkɑŋgrɪˈgeɪʃən/ n.

a group of people who adhere to a common faith and habitually attend a given church （教堂里的）集会；集合

low-brow /ˈləʊbraʊ/ adj.

low-brow entertainment, newspapers, books etc. are easy to understand and are not concerned with serious ideas about art, culture, etc. — used to show disapproval 庸俗的；低俗的

superfluity /ˌsuːpə(r)ˈfluətɪ/ n.

extreme excess 过剩；多余物

captive audience

people who listen or watch sb. or sth. because they have to, not because they are interested 受制而走不开的听众

Suggested Topics for Writing

1. Do you agree that the function of education is to prepare us for life? Use specific reasons to explain your answer.

2. "If our schools teach nothing else, they should at least teach critical thinking." To what extent do you agree or disagree with the quotation?

(选文:任爱军;注释:管琛)

Unit Eleven Culture Studies

1. *Lost in Thailand*: Did China's Comedy Hit Get Lost in Translation?

By Phil Hoad[1]

1 ① A whiff of revolution was in the air last weekend; could it be that it was coming from that new low-budget Chinese comedy? But *Lost in Thailand*, opening in a mere 29 out of America's 5,000 cinemas, was no ordinary Chinese comedy. Called China's answer to *The Hangover*[2], the $3m (£1.9m) chancer knocked *Life of Pi* off China's No. 1 spot in December and surprised several domestic blockbusters on its way to becoming their most successful film ever — homegrown or foreign. Something unspoken lay behind expectant articles in the film press for its U.S. opening; the idea that this could be the point when cinema's trade winds stopped blowing from west to east, and the reverse became possible.

2 Well, sorry, not quite. Not even Chinese-Americans represented in serious numbers, given this auspicious opportunity; *Lost in Thailand* took only $29,143 over the weekend (a moderate screen average of $833), to boost its record-breaking $194m Chinese haul. ② It's a blow for those interested observers who had noted that this unexpected hit from a minor studio was a very different breed of Sino-blockbuster. It wasn't the normal sensational historical

epic or martial-arts fantasia, but a skillful contemporary comedy in which a businessman (Xu Zheng, who also directs) trying to track down his boss in Thailand is frustrated by a Zach Galifianakis[3]-like buffoon (Wang Baoqiang). (Technically, it's more Chinese *Due Date*[4] than *The Hangover*.)

3   *Lost in Thailand* touched on an open contemporary nerve rarely visible in the country's commercial cinema. It's been praised for speaking directly to the ambitions and anxieties of China's growing urban middle class. "Many of them feel confused and tired and even like they are losing themselves," Beijing university's Zhang Yiwu told the *South China Morning Post*, "*Lost in Thailand* is a very good movie for invoking thought and showing the frailty of urban citizens." ③ Invoking thought wasn't something *The Hangover*, or many of the other mismatched-buddy Hollywood models for *Lost in Thailand* (the Zheng-Baoqiang partnership was first struck up in 2010's *Lost on Journey*, apparently inspired by *Planes, Trains and Automobiles*[5]), were remembered for — but then this style of film is still a novelty for Chinese audiences.

4   The hope was that this new vein of comedy, and the resulting boost to the industry's self-confidence, would impress the other side of the world; that it would prove Chinese cinema was finally gaining the kind of the spirit needed to be truly responsive and commercial. Then the unimaginable — that the country's film-makers would one day challenge Hollywood for global influence — might look plausible. But cinema chain AMC's decision to treat *Lost in Thailand* as just another niche release means that the new face of Chinese film (if there is one) remains untested in this biggest of arenas. It's possible, of course, that AMC (who acted, unusually as both distributor and exhibitor) made a prudent market call, and *Lost in Thailand*'s humour is simply too Chinese to gain wider sway. ④ That was presumably the case with the entertaining but often confusing 2010 action-comedy *Let the Bullets Fly*, another former Chinese No. 1, which grossed a feeble $69,000 in the States.

5   ⑤ I don't buy the argument that any film is "too culturally [whatever]" to

succeed — the east, with China catching up over the last decade, has been lapping up Hollywood and American values for half a century, and there's no innate reason the opposite won't happen. Chinese culture overall might have to start looking a bit more comely first; there might have to be a few more *Lost in Thailands* to break in western audiences. Perhaps Xu Zheng's comedy needs time to freshen up the Chinese industry internally for those things to happen. Hollywood might have got a reprieve from that particular hangover for a couple more years.

(From *The Guardian*, February 13, 2013)

Notes

[1] **Phil Hoad**: A freelance journalist specializing in the globalization of cinema. He has written for *The Guardian*, *The Observer*, *Al-Jazeera*, *The Independent*, *The Big Issue and Dazed & Confused*.

[2] ***The Hangover***: It is a 2009 American comedy film directed by Todd Phillips, co-produced with Daniel Goldberg, and written by Jon Lucas and Scott Moore. The film stars Bradley Cooper, Ed Helms, Zach Galifianakis, Heather Graham, Ken Jeong, Rachael Harris, Mike Epps, Justin Bartha, and Jeffrey Tambor. It tells the story of Phil Wenneck, Stu Price, Alan Garner, and Doug Billings, who travel to Las Vegas for a bachelor party to celebrate Doug's impending marriage. However, Phil, Stu and Alan wake up with Doug missing and no memory of the previous night's events, and must find the groom before the wedding can take place.

[3] **Zach Galifianakis**: An American actor, writer and comedian. He came to prominence with his Comedy Central Presents special in 2001 and presented his own show called *Late World with Zach* on VH1 the following year. He has also starred in films, such as *The Hangover trilogy* (2009—2013), *Due Date* (2010), *The Campaign* (2012), *Birdman* (2014), *Puss in Boots* (2011),

Masterminds (2016) *and The Lego Batman Movie* (2017).

[4] ***Due Date***: It is a 2010 American comedy film directed by Todd Phillips, co-written by Alan R. Cohen, Alan Freedland, and Adam Sztykiel, and starring Robert Downey, Jr. and Zach Galifianakis. The film was released on November 5, 2010. The film was shot in Las Cruces, New Mexico, Atlanta, Georgia, and Tuscaloosa, Alabama.

[5] ***Planes, Trains and Automobiles***: It is a 1987 American comedy film written, produced and directed by John Hughes. The film stars Steve Martin as Neal Page, a high-strung marketing executive, who meets Del Griffith, played by John Candy, an eternally optimistic, outgoing, overly talkative, and clumsy shower curtain ring salesman. They share a three-day odyssey of misadventures trying to get Neal home to Chicago from New York City in time for Thanksgiving with his family.

Words and Phrases

chancer /ˈtʃɑːnsə(r)/ *n.*
someone to takes risks in the interest of personal gain 敢冒任何风险的人；投机分子

auspicious /ɔːˈspɪʃəs/ *adj.*
showing signs that suggest that something is likely to be successful 吉利的

buffoon /bəˈfuːn/ *n.*
a person who does silly but amusing things 小丑；滑稽可笑的人

invoke /ɪnˈvəʊk/ *v.*
to make sb. have a particular feeling or imagine a particular scene 唤起；引起

frailty /ˈfreɪlti/
weakness and poor health 虚弱；衰弱

vein /veɪn/ *n.*

a particular style or manner   风格；方式

plausible /ˈplɔːzəbl/ *adj.*

reasonable and likely to be true   有道理的；可信的

niche /nɪtʃ/ *n.*

an opportunity to sell a particular product to a particular group of people   商机；市场定位

gross /grəʊs/ *v.*

to earn a particular amount of money before taxes or costs have been taken out（未扣除各项费用之前）总共赚得

publicity /pʌbˈlɪsəti/ *n.*

the business of attracting the attention of the public   广告宣传工作

train /treɪn/ *v.*

to aim something such as a weapon or camera at somebody or something   瞄准

diverge /daɪˈvɜːdʒ/ *v.*

to separate and go in different directions   分叉；岔开

comely /ˈkʌmli/ *adj.*

pleasant to look at   标致的；秀丽的

reprieve /rɪˈpriːv/ *n.*

the halting or delay of somebody's punishment, especially when the punishment is death   缓刑

trade winds

strong winds that blow all the time towards the equator and then to the west   信风；贸易风

track down

to find a person, animal, or object by searching or following a trail   追踪

strike up

to begin something, or cause something to begin   开始

gain sway

    to get ruling or controlling power　获得影响力

lap up

    to catch up　追赶

freshen up

    to increase in strength　振作

Reading Comprehension Questions

1. In the film press for its U. S. opening, the expectant articles expressed implicitly that _____.

    (A) Chinese films will go into the world

    (B) American films will occupy China's market

    (C) there will probably be a new trend in the film business

    (D) films from the western countries will be forbidden in China

2. *Lost in Thailand* is concerned with the topic about _____.

    (A) the confusion and tiredness of China's urban middle class

    (B) the failure of urban citizens

    (C) the fact that people are losing confidence in their boss

    (D) Chinese films going into the world market

3. It appears that so far Chinese films in American market _____.

    (A) have left a deep impression on the film watchers

    (B) show signs to challenge Hollywood

    (C) will have global influence as is the case with *Let the Bullets Fly*

    (D) are not winning audience because of cultural differences

4. Concerning the publicity of *Lost in Thailand*, _____.

    (A) Dalian Wanda Group has not made enough efforts

    (B) there is little YouTube and Facebook

    (C) the Chinese government has offered support

(D) AMC has shown muscle

5. The author of the article seems to believe that _____.

(A) Chinese culture is reason for China's film to succeed in America

(B) Hollywood is not facing the competition from China now

(C) Chinese culture will be more comely in a couple of years

(D) Xu Zheng needs more time to produce more films like *Lost in Thailand*

(选文:陈馥梅;注释:徐守平)

2. Preserve the Country's Own Culture

By Mohan Sivanand[1]

Can a country protect and preserve its own culture when it's constantly exposed to foreign influences? Our Indian edition editor Mohan Sivanand says yes!

1   I live in Mumbai[2], India, a big city, but I'm acutely aware that I came from a remote Kerala village. When I was a boy, hardly anyone spoke English around me. So, at age nine, Dad decided to pack me off to Montfort, a boarding school in another state. There, I had to speak English or be punished. ① I wore grey flannels, blazer and tie, and played cricket — so different from Kerala in the 1960s, where little boys went around in shorts and half-sleeved shirts that were never tucked in. The men wore dhotis, a traditional Indian garment. Villagers walked barefoot or wore slippers, but nobody had shoes. As for cricket, hardly anyone had heard about that English game.

2   My boarding school, nestled amid pines and silver oaks, was once meant to be a home away from home for the children of British officers serving in India.

3   By the time I joined in 1961, nearly all the boys attending Monfort were Indian, but many English traditions continued to live on. ② At the end of the school year, when I went home for the holidays, I must have forgotten local dress codes. Everybody was staring at me — just because I came back in shoes and slacks. "Sahib!" one or two local boys hissed, the word used for lordly Brits who once ruled India.

4   "Hey you, speak some English," some of my neighbours used to tell me, half in jest. Looking back, I think I unwittingly brought a bit of English culture

to my village.

5   But English and too much Western influence are precisely what many traditionalists and political leaders fear. They ask: Will such influences distort or finish off our own culture?

6   Some Indian leaders have tried very hard to erase our colonial legacy. They've pulled down old British statues and replaced many colonial city names like Bombay and Calcutta with older native names, Mumbai or Kolkata[3]. British street names too are disappearing. Diehard nationalists have even suggested we make Tuesday, the Hindu holy day, our weekly day of rest instead of the "Western" Sunday.

7   ③ Extreme responses I say. You can't alter history, and it is only natural for foreign influences to permeate a nation's culture. So Indian culture, as it is today, is really a hybrid derived from centuries of Aryan, Greek, Afghan, Moghul and European invasions.

8   Add to that the massive changes of the 20th century resulting from the semi-conductor revolution, the pill, jet-age travel, the Internet, etc.

9   Everything from clothes and language to food keeps changing, yet we remain every bit Indian and Asian. I believe that Asian cultures, like Indian, are too ancient and deep-rooted to be distorted by any kind of foreign influence.

10   Allow me to illustrate my point. ④ Some time ago my wife Sheila and I took a close relative, who was visiting us from Singapore, to a Chinese restaurant in Mumbai. The relative, born and bred in Singapore and who often enjoyed cooking Chinese delicacies for his daughters, ate a full dinner of sweet-corn soup, fried rice, chicken chilli fry with us. Later, while driving home, I talked about the fine Chinese food we'd just had.

11   "Was that Chinese food?" our guest exclaimed innocently. "Oh, I didn't know." It must have tasted too Indian for him to realise it.

12   Meanwhile, like countless other Asian villages, my rural community in Kerala has transformed over the past decades. Lots of people wear shoes and

trousers — even some of the girls. Cable TV brings live cricket to drawing rooms and playgrounds and even village elders follow every major match. ⑤ There's also an English-medium co-ed boarding school run by missionaries, just a five-minute stroll from my home. There, you overhear the kids giggling, yelling, flirting — all in English, but with an Indian accent, often mixed with local touches. Just like the Chinese or Italian food you get in India.

13 Are these foreign influences something we should be worried about? I don't think so. Chinese food in India tastes pretty good to me!

(From *Reader's Digest*. https://zh. scribd. com/document/106213708/Preserve-the-Country)

Notes

[1] **Mohan Sivanand**(1951 –): Born in Kerala India, an Indian journalist and artist. For a decade, until October 2015, he was Editor-in-Chief of the Indian edition of *Reader's Digest*. Sivanand started drawing while at college in Kerala, publishing his first cartoon in Shankar's Weekly, India's equivalent of *Punch*, in 1975. After graduate studies in journalism, he worked for *The Times* of India group in Bombay, where his cartoons and articles appeared regularly in several of the group's publications. He was on the editorial staff of *Science Today* magazine for over five years. Sivanand has won the Malayala Manorama-instituted "K. M. Cheriyan Memorial Gold Medal" in 1975, after topping his class at the Institute of Journalism, Trivandrum, Kerala, where he did graduate studies. He also won a "Rajika Kripalani Young Journalist of the Year Award" in 1979.

[2] **Mumbai**: Formerly Bombay, city, capital of Maharashtra state, southwestern India. It is the country's financial and commercial centre and its principal port on the Arabian Sea.

[3] **Kolkata**: Bengali Kalikata, formerly Calcutta, city, capital of West

Bengal state, and former capital (1772 - 1911) of British India. It is one of India's largest cities and one of its major ports.

Words and Phrases

flannels /ˈflænlz/ *n.*

trousers/ pants made of flannel 法兰绒裤

dhoti /ˈdəʊti/ *n.*

a garment worn by male Hindus, consisting of a piece of material tied around the waist and extending to cover most of the legs 印度男子的多蒂腰布

garment /ˈɡɑːmənt/ *n.*

a piece of clothing 衣服

nestle /ˈnesl/ *prep.*

to be located in a position that is protected, sheltered or partly hidden 坐落；位于

unwittingly /ʌnˈwɪtɪŋli/ *adv.*

without being aware of what you are doing or of the situation you are involved in 无意地

legacy /ˈleɡəsi/ *n.*

a situation that exists now because of events, actions, etc. that took place in the past 遗留问题

diehard /ˈdaɪhɑːd/ *adj.*

strongly opposing change and new ideas 顽固的；因循守旧的

permeate /ˈpɜːmieɪt/ *v.*

(of an idea, an influence, a feeling, etc.) to affect every part of something 感染；传播；扩散

hybrid /ˈhaɪbrɪd/ *n.*

something that is the product of mixing two or more different things 混合物

distort (sth.) /dɪˈstɔːt/ *v.*

to twist or change facts, ideas, etc. so that they are no longer correct or true

歪曲；曲解

delicacy /ˈdelɪkəsi/ n.

a type of food considered to be very special in a particular place 佳肴

missionary /ˈmɪʃəneri/ n.

a person who is sent to a foreign country to teach people about Christianity 传教士

stroll /strəʊl/ v.

walk leisurely and with no apparent aim 漫步

overhear /ˌəʊvəˈhɪə(r)/ v.

to hear, especially by accident, a conversation in which you are not involved 偶然听到；无意中听到

pack off

to send somebody somewhere, especially because you do not want them with you 把……打发走

tuck in

to push, fold or turn the ends or edges of clothes, paper, etc. so that they are held in place or look neat 塞进

in jest

as a joke 开玩笑地

finish off

to destroy somebody/ something, especially somebody/ something that is badly injured or damaged 彻底摧毁

result from

to happen because of something else that happened first 随……产生；因……发生

Suggested Topics for Writing

1. Can a country protect and preserve its own culture when it's constantly exposed to foreign influences? Use specific reasons and details to support your answer.

2. Do you agree or disagree with the following statement? Chinese culture is too ancient and deep-rooted to be distorted by any kind of foreign influences. Use specific reasons and details to develop your essay.

(选文:任爱军;注释:何朝阳)

Unit Twelve   New Insight

1. Why Waiting Is Torture

By Alex Stone[1]

1   Some years ago, executives at a Houston airport faced a troubling customer-relations issue. Passengers were lodging an inordinate number of complaints about the long waits at baggage claim. In response, the executives increased the number of baggage handlers working that shift. The plan worked: the average wait fell to eight minutes, well within industry benchmarks. But the complaints persisted.

2   Puzzled, the airport executives undertook a more careful, on-site analysis. They found that it took passengers a minute to walk from their arrival gates to baggage claim and seven more minutes to get their bags. Roughly 88 percent of their time, in other words, was spent standing around waiting for their bags.

3   So the airport decided on a new approach: instead of reducing wait times, it moved the arrival gates away from the main terminal and routed bags to the outermost carousel. Passengers now had to walk six times longer to get their bags. Complaints dropped to near zero.

4   ① This story hints at a general principle: the experience of waiting, whether for luggage or groceries, is defined only partly by the objective length of the wait. "Often the psychology of queuing is more important than the statistics of the wait itself," notes the MIT[2] operations researcher Richard

Larson, widely considered to be the world's foremost expert on lines. Occupied time (walking to baggage claim) feels shorter than unoccupied time (standing at the carousel). Research on queuing has shown that, on average, people overestimate how long they've waited in a line by about 36 percent.

5   This is also why one finds mirrors next to elevators. The idea was born during the post-World War II boom[3], when the spread of high-rises led to complaints about elevator delays. The rationale behind the mirrors was similar to the one used at the Houston airport: give people something to occupy their time, and the wait will feel shorter. With the mirrors, people could check their hair or slyly ogle other passengers. And it worked: almost overnight, the complaints ceased.

6   The drudgery of unoccupied time also accounts in large measure for the popularity of impulse-buy items, which earn supermarkets about $5.5 billion annually. The tabloids and packs of gum offer relief from the agony of waiting.

7   ② Our expectations further affect how we feel about lines. Uncertainty magnifies the stress of waiting, while feedback in the form of expected wait times and explanations for delays improves the tenor of the experience.

8   And beating expectations buoys our mood. All else being equal, people who wait less than they anticipated leave happier than those who wait longer than expected. This is why Disney, the universally acknowledged master of applied queuing psychology, overestimates waiting time for rides, so that its guests — never customers, always guests — are pleasantly surprised when they ascend Space Mountain ahead of schedule.

9   This is a powerful ploy because our memories of a queuing experience, to use an industry term, are strongly influenced by the final moments, according to research conducted by Ziv Carmon, a professor of marketing at the business school INSEAD, and the behavioral economist Daniel Kahneman. When a long wait ends on a happy note — the line speeds up, say — we tend to look back on it positively, even if we were miserable much of the time. Conversely, if negative emotions dominate in the final minutes, our retrospective audit of the

process will skew toward cynicism, even if the experience as a whole was relatively painless.

10 Professors Carmon and Kahneman have also found that we are more concerned with how long a line is than how fast it's moving. Given a choice between a slow-moving short line and a fast-moving long one, we will often opt for the former, even if the waits are identical. (This is why Disney hides the lengths of its lines by wrapping them around buildings and using serpentine queues.)

11 ③ <u>Perhaps the biggest influence on our feelings about lines, though, has to do with our perception of fairness. When it comes to lines, the universally acknowledged standard is first come first served; any deviation is, to most, a mark of iniquity and can lead to violent queue rage.</u> Last month a man was stabbed at a Maryland post office by a fellow customer who mistakenly thought he'd cut in line. Professor Larson calls these unwelcome intrusions "slips" and "skips".

12 ④ <u>The demand for fairness extends beyond mere self-interest. Like any social system, lines are governed by an implicit set of norms that transcend the individual.</u> A study of fans in line for U2 tickets found that people are just as upset by slips and skips that occur behind them, and thus don't lengthen their wait, as they are by those in front of them.

13 Surveys show that many people will wait twice as long for fast food, provided the establishment uses a first-come-first-served, single-queue ordering system as opposed to a multi-queue setup. Anyone who's ever had to choose a line at a grocery store knows how unfair multiple queues can seem; invariably, you wind up kicking yourself for not choosing the line next to you moving twice as fast.

14 But there's a curious cognitive asymmetry at work here. While losing to the line at our left drives us to despair, winning the race against the one to our right does little to lift our spirits. Indeed, in a system of multiple queues, customers almost always fixate on the line they're losing to and rarely the one

they're beating.

15 Fairness also dictates that the length of a line should be commensurate with the value of the product or service for which we're waiting. The more valuable it is, the longer one is willing to wait for it. Hence the supermarket express line, a rare, socially sanctioned violation of first come first served, based on the assumption that no reasonable person thinks a child buying a candy bar should wait behind an old man stocking up on provisions for the Mayan apocalypse.

16 Americans spend roughly 37 billion hours each year waiting in line. ⑤ The dominant cost of waiting is an emotional one: stress, boredom, that nagging sensation that one's life is slipping away. The last thing we want to do with our dwindling leisure time is squander it in stasis. We'll never eliminate lines altogether, but a better understanding of the psychology of waiting can help make those inevitable delays that inject themselves into our daily lives a touch more bearable. And when all else fails, bring a book.

(From *The New York Times*. August 19, 2012.)

Notes

[1] **Alex Stone**: a Los Angeles-based national correspondent for ABC News Radio. Since joining ABC News, Stone has covered stories around the globe, including the 2004 Southeast Asia tsunami and the 2011 Japan earthquake and tsunami. He traveled to Beijing to cover the 2008 Summer Olympics, Vancouver for the 2010 Winter Olympics, and London for the 2012 Summer Olympics. In 2005 Stone spent weeks in New Orleans and the surrounding areas of Louisiana covering Hurricane Katrina and the storm's aftermath. He has also covered numerous high profile trials for ABC News, including the cases of Scott Peterson, Kobe Bryant, Michael Jackson and OJ Simpson.

[2] **MIT**: Massachusetts Institute of Technology (麻省理工学院).

[3] **Post-World War Ⅱ Boom**: The end of World War Ⅱ brought a baby boom to many countries, especially Western ones. In May 1951, Sylvia Porter, a columnist for *the New York Post*, used the term "boom" to refer to the phenomenon of increased births in post war America.

Words and Phrases

lodge /lɒdʒ/ *v.*
 lodge sth. (with sb.) (against sb./sth.) to make a formal statement about something to a public organization or authority　提出（报告、要求、申诉等）

inordinate /ɪnˈɔːdɪnət/ *adj.*
 far more than what is usual or expected　无节制的；过度的

benchmark /ˈbentʃmɑːk/ *n.*
 something that can be measured and used as a standard that other things can be compared with　基准；行业标准

route /ruːt/ *v.*
 to send somebody/something by a particular route　按某路线发送

carousel /ˌkærəˈsel/ *n.*
 a moving belt from which you collect your bags at an airport　行李传送带

high-rise /haɪˈraɪz/ *n.*
 a building that is very tall and has a lot of floors　高楼；多层建筑物

rationale /ˌræʃəˈnɑːl/ *n.*
 the principles or reasons which explain a particular decision, course of action, belief, etc.　基本原理；根据

ogle /ˈəʊɡl/ *v.*
 to look hard at somebody in an offensive way, usually showing sexual interest　（向……）抛媚眼；送秋波

drudgery /ˈdrʌdʒəri/ *n.*
 hard boring work　单调沉闷的工作

agony /ˈæɡəni/ *n.*

extreme physical or mental pain 极大的痛苦;苦恼

tenor /ˈtenə(r)/ *n*.

the general character or meaning of something 大意;要旨

ploy /plɔɪ/ *n*.

words or actions that are carefully planned to get an advantage over somebody else 策略;手法

retrospective /ˌretrəˈspektɪv/ *adj*.

thinking about or connected with something that happened in the past 回顾;追溯

audit /ˈɔːdɪt/ *n*.

an official examination of the quality or standard of something 审计;查账

skew /skjuː/ *v*.

to move or lie at an angle, especially in a position that is not normal 偏离;歪斜

cynicism /ˈsɪnɪsɪzəm/ *n*.

the belief that something good will not happen or that something is not important 玩世不恭;愤世嫉俗

serpentine /ˈsɜːpəntaɪn/ *adj*.

bending and twisting like a snake 像蛇般蜷曲的;蜿蜒的

iniquity /ɪˈnɪkwəti/ *n*.

the fact of being very unfair or wrong; something that is very unfair or wrong 极不公正;邪恶

transcend /trænˈsend/ *v*.

to be or go beyond the usual limits of something 超越;超出……的限度

cognitive /ˈkɒɡnətɪv/ *adj*.

connected with mental processes of understanding 认知的

asymmetry /eɪˈsɪmətrɪ/ *n*.

the quality of having two sides or parts that are not the same in size or shape 不对称

fixate /ˈfɪkseɪt/ *v*.

cause (someone) to develop an obsessive attachment to someone or something 注视;定睛于;使固定

commensurate /kəˈmenʃərət/ *adj.*

matching something in size, importance, quality, etc. （在时间和空间上）相等的;相称的

sanction /ˈsæŋkʃn/ *v.*

to give permission for something to take place 批准

nagging /ˈnæɡɪŋ/ *adj.*

complaining 抱怨的;挑剔的

dwindle /ˈdwɪndl/ *v.*

to become gradually less or smaller 减少;变小;缩小

squander /ˈskwɒndə(r)/ *v.*

to waste money, time, etc. in a stupid or careless way 挥霍;浪费

stasis /ˈsteɪsɪs/ *n.*

a situation in which there is no change or development 停滞;郁积

buoy sb.（up）

to make somebody feel cheerful or confident 鼓励;打气

wind up

(of a person) to find yourself in a particular place or situation 使结束;收尾

Reading Comprehension Questions

1. What can we infer from the airport story? _____

   (A) People tend to be worried about waiting no matter what length the time is.

   (B) People want to get their best service instantly.

   (C) People need something to distract them from their waiting time.

   (D) People feel impatient because they overestimate the time spent on waiting.

2. According to the passage, the main cause for people to buy items on impulse

is _____.

(A) the attraction of items themselves

(B) the sales promotion

(C) the killing of unoccupied time

(D) the desire to keep up with the Jones'

3. The measures Disney takes to avoid guests' impatience at queuing include all the following except that they _____.

(A) overestimate waiting time so people feel happier when they really wait less than they anticipate

(B) try to speed up the queue so people can move faster

(C) make guests final experience happy to payoff their waiting time

(D) hide the lengths of the waiting lines so that they seem not so long

4. "Slips" and "Skips" are considered unwelcome intrusions because they _____.

(A) violate the social demand for fairness: first come first served

(B) make people behind wait longer than they have expected

(C) behave rude and make people in line feel unhappy

(D) show kind of self-interest and no consideration of those in line

5. The author suggests that understanding the psychology of waiting can help us _____.

(A) solve the boredom of queuing

(B) reduce compliant claims about waiting too long

(C) bear with those unavoidable waiting time in life

(D) avoid waiting as a tortuous experience

(选文、注释:丁菲菲)

2. Pathways Seen For Acquiring Languages

By Sarah D. Sparks

1   New studies on how language learning occurs are beginning to chip away at some long-held notions about second-language acquisition and point to potential learning benefits for students who speak more than one language.

2   "We have this national psyche that we're not good at languages," said Marty Abbott, the director of education for the American Council on the Teaching of Foreign Languages (ACTFL)[1], in Alexandria, Va. "It's still perceived as something only smart people can do, and it's not true; we all learned our first language and we can learn a second one."

3   New National Science Foundation (NSF)[2]— funded collaborations among educators, cognitive scientists, neuroscientists, psychologists, and linguists have started to find the evidence to back up that assertion. ① <u>For example, researchers long thought the window for learning a new language shrinks rapidly after age 7 and closes almost entirely after puberty. Yet interdisciplinary research conducted over the past five years at the University of Washington, Pennsylvania State University, and other colleges suggest that the time frame may be more flexible than first thought and that students who learn additional languages become more adaptable in other types of learning, too.</u>

4   "There has been an explosion of research on bilingual-language processing," said Judith F. Kroll, the principal investigator for the Bilingualism, Mind, and Brain project launched this month at Penn State's Center for Language Science in University Park, Pa. The five-year, $2.8 million project is intended to bring together neuroscientists, linguists, and cognitive scientists to compare the brain and mental processes of different types

of bilingual people, such as a Mandarin-English speaker whose languages include different writing systems or a deaf English speaker whose signed and written languages involve different modes of communication.

5   Likewise, the Washington-based American Association for the Advancement of Science (AAAS)[3] has added a symposium on bilingualism to its 2011 annual conference in February, and the Seattle-based University of Washington this May opened the world's first brain-imaging center adapted to study language and cognition in infants and young children.

6   ② "Bilingualism provides a lens for researchers to examine aspects of the underlying cognitive architecture that are otherwise obscured by native-language skills," Ms. Kroll said.

New Techniques

7   The increased use of neuroscience in language-acquisition research has been fueled in part by the development of brain-imaging equipment scaled for tiny brains and squirmy bodies, according to Patricia K. Kuhl, a co-director of the University of Washington's Institute for Learning and Brain Sciences, known as I-LABS. The technology has enabled scientists over the past decade to start to paint a picture of how language learning affects a child's brain.

8   Among the new techniques is magnetoencephalography, or MEG, which maps brain activity by measuring the magnetic fields produced by the brain's electrical currents. The I-LABS machine's sensors use a unique global positioning system to correct the resulting image for the child's head movements.

9   In a series of experiments, Ms. Kuhl and her team studied American infants of English-speaking parents between the ages of 6 and 12 months. During the first year, the team found the auditory and motor regions of the brain start to react more in response to speech, as opposed to other sound. "They are mapping the language, so the faster they can map those critical sounds, the faster their language is going to grow," she said. "Babies start out

as citizens of the world; they can discriminate the sounds of any language."

10   Yet during about a two-month window from 8- to 10-months-old, the team found babies start to specialize in sounds from their native language. For instance, an English-speaking baby will get better at hearing the difference between the often-used "l" and "r" sounds, while a Japanese baby, whose native language does not differentiate between the sounds, will get worse at hearing the difference.

11   Since the initial experiments, the researchers have drilled down into exactly what sort of experience props open that language-learning window.

12   For example, when babies born to native English-speaking parents played three times a week during that window with a native Mandarin-speaking tutor, at 12 months, they had progressed in their ability to recognize both English and Mandarin sounds, rather than starting to retrench in the non-native language. By contrast, children exposed only to audio or video recordings of native speakers showed no change in their language trajectory. Brain-imaging of the same children backed up the results of test-based measures of language specialization.

13   ③ The research may not immediately translate into a new language arts curriculum, but it has already deepened the evidence for something most educators believe: Social engagement, particularly with speakers of multiple languages, is critical to language learning. Social and emotional areas of the brain mediate language areas, but only now—with a MEG that can correct for the child's head movement—are researchers starting to measure those neural connections.

14   "When we can connect language regions with social-emotional regions with executive functions, we'll have a picture of the whole system," said Gina C. Lebedeva, the translation outreach and education director for I-LABS.

15   "The key to that series of studies is exposure and live interactions with native speakers," Ms. Lebedeva said. "The interactions need to be naturalistic: eye contact, gestures, exaggerated phonemes."

Earlier Exposure

16 With the opening this summer of I-LABS' $7 million MEG brain imaging center, Ms. Kuhl and lab co-director Andrew Meltzoff will launch a new phase of research. The Developing Mind Project is studying how people's brain and cognitive processes change during key transition periods: infancy and early childhood, puberty, and old age.

17 Ms. Abbott said she hopes such research will help persuade education officials to provide more second-language instruction for all students in early grades, as opposed to the traditional secondary school courses.

18 "Just around the time when most students in this country, if they study a language, are starting that process, they're becoming less likely to be able to make those native-like sounds in another language," Ms. Abbott said.

19 ④ <u>Ms. Kuhl and Ms. Lebedeva agreed. "I think we may be able to draw a new language learning curve that's not so age-dependent," Ms. Kuhl said. "Learning itself in early development is so profound, and the neural architecture stays with you throughout your life."</u>

20 Other studies also suggest that learning multiple languages from early childhood on may provide broader academic benefits, too.

21 For example, at the science-oriented Ultimate Block Party held in New York City this month, children of different backgrounds played games in which they were required to sort toys either by shape or color, based on a rule indicated by changing flashcards. ⑤ <u>A child sorting blue and yellow ducks and trucks by shape, say, might suddenly have to switch to sorting them by color. The field games exemplified research findings that bilingual children have greater cognitive flexibility than monolingual children. That is, they can adapt better than monolingual children to changes in rules, for example, the criteria used to sort the toys, and close out mental distractions.</u>

(From *Education Week*, October 27, 2010)

Notes

[1] **The American Council on the Teaching of Foreign Languages (ACTFL)**: An American organization aiming to improve and expand the teaching and learning of all languages at all levels of instruction. ACTFL is an individual membership organization of more than 12,500 foreign language educators and administrators from elementary through graduate education, as well as in government and industry.

[2] **The National Science Foundation (NSF)**: A U.S. government agency that supports fundamental research and education in all the non-medical fields of science and engineering. Its medical counterpart is the National Institute of Health. With an annual budget of about U.S. $7 billion (fiscal year 2012), the NSF funds approximately 24% of all federally supported basic research conducted by the U.S. colleges and universities. In some fields, such as mathematics, computer science, economics and the social sciences, the NSF is the major source of federal backing.

[3] **The American Association for the Advancement of Science (AAAS)**: An American international non-profit organization with the stated goals of promoting cooperation among scientists, defending scientific freedom, encouraging scientific responsibility, and supporting scientific education and science outreach for the betterment of all humanity. It is the world's largest general scientific society, with 126,995 individual and institutional members at the end of 2008, and is the publisher of the well-known scientific journal *Science*, which has a weekly circulation of 138,549.

Words and Phrases

psyche /ˈsaɪki/ *n.*

 the mind; your deepest feelings and attitudes 心灵;心态

cognitive /ˈkɒgnətɪv/ *n.*

  connected with mental processes of understanding   认知的；感知的

neuroscientist /ˈnjʊərəʊsaɪəntɪst/   *n.*

  a person engaged in the study of science that deals with the structure and function of the brain and the nervous system   神经科学专家

assertion /əˈsɜːʃn/   *n.*

  a statement saying that you strongly believe sth. to be true   认定；断言

interdisciplinary /ˌɪntəˈdɪsəplɪnəri/   *adj.*

  involving different areas of knowledge or study   多学科的；跨学科的

bilingual /baɪˈlɪŋgwəl/   *adj.*

  able to speak two languages; using two languages   会说两种语言的；用两种语言的

symposium /sɪmˈpəʊziəm/   *n.*

  a meeting at which experts have discussions about a particular subject; a small conference   专题讨论会；小型讨论会

scale /skeɪl/   *v.*

  to make writing or a picture the right size for a particular purpose   改变大小；调整大小

squirmy /ˈskwɜːmi/   *adj.*

  twisting your body from side to side because you are uncomfortable or nervous   蠕动的；不安的

auditory /ˈɔːdətri/   *adj.*

  connected with hearing   听觉的；听的

motor /ˈməʊtə(k)/   *adj.*

  connected with the nerves that control movement   运动神经的

map /mæp/   *v.*

  to discover or give information about sth., especially the way it is arranged or organized   了解/提供信息（尤指其编排或组织方式）

discriminate /dɪˈskrɪmɪneɪt/   *v.*

  to recognize that there's a difference between people or things   区别；辨别；

区分

differentiate /ˌdɪfəˈrenʃieɪt/ *v.*

to recognize or show that two things are not the same 区分;区别;辨别

Mandarin /ˈmændərɪn/ *n.*

the standard form of Chinese 普通话

retrench /rɪˈtrentʃ/ *v.*

to spend less money or reduce costs 节约;紧缩开支

trajectory /trəˈdʒektərɪ/ *n.*

the curved path of sth. that has been fired, hit or thrown into the air 轨道;轨迹;弹道

mediate /ˈmiːdieɪt/ *v.*

to influence sth. and make it possible to happen 影响并致其发生

neural /ˈnjʊərəl/ *adj.*

connected with a nerve or the nervous system 神经的;神经系统的

outreach /ˈaʊtriːtʃ/ *n.*

an activity of an organization that provides a service or advice to people who would not otherwise get these services easily 扩大服务范围

phoneme /ˈfəʊniːm/ *n.*

any one of the set of smallest units of speech in a language that distinguish one word from another 音位;音素

flashcard /ˈflæʃkɑːd/ *n.*

a card with a word or picture on it, that teachers use during lesson 教学卡片;识字卡

exemplify /ɪɡˈzemplɪfaɪ/ *v.*

to give an example in order to make sth. clearer 例示;例证

chip away at

to gradually make sth. less effective, weaker or destroy it 冲击;削弱

as opposed to

used to make a contrast between two things 而;相对于

prop open

    to open sth. and keep it in that position 支开

close out

    to finish or settle sth. 结束；了结

Suggested Topics for Writing

1. Some people believe that it's more important for young children to go to a bilingual kindergarten where both Chinese and English are spoken than to attend an all-Chinese kindergarten. What do you think? Use specific reasons and examples to support your opinion.

2. Some people believe that college English learning should be optional rather than compulsory on school curriculum. What's your opinion? Use specific reasons and examples to support your answer.

(选文、注释：薛光荣)

Unit Thirteen　Personality and Character

1. The Ungrateful President

By Maureen Dowd[1]

1　At a fund-raiser for the president at his Westport, Connecticut, estate Monday night, Harvey Weinstein spoke in a softly lit room shimmering with pink dahlias, gold Oscars, silvery celebrities and black American Express cards.

2　"You can make the case," Weinstein said of Barack Obama, "that he's the Paul Leonard Newman[2] of American presidents."

3　I interviewed Paul Newman. I knew Paul Newman. Paul Newman was an acquaintance of mine. Mr. President, except for the eyes, you are sort of like Paul Newman.

4　"I've been accused of being aloof," Newman told me. "I'm not. I'm just wary."

5　The star scorned the hoops he was expected to jump through in his profession and did not like feeling beholden. He said he dealt with fame by developing "selective insensitivities".

6　① "With film critics and fans, you have to be selectively insensitive to their insensitivities," he told me. "If people start treating you like a piece of meat or a long-lost friend or feel they can become cuddly for the price of a $5 movie ticket, then you shut them out."

7　Just so, the president does not think people should expect too much in return for paying $35,800 for an hour of his time, as they did at the Weinstein affair, or in return for other favors.

8   ② <u>Obama smashed through all the barriers and dysfunction in his life to become a self-made, self-narrating president. His brash 2008 campaign invented a new blueprint to upend the Democratic establishment. So it's understandable if Obama, with his Shaker aesthetic, is not inclined to play by the rococo rules of politics. Yet, as the president struggles to stay ahead of Moneybags Romney, his selective insensitivities may be hurting him.</u>

9   Stories abound of big donors who stopped giving as much or working as hard because Obama never reached out, either with a Clinton-esque warm bath of attention or Romney-esque weekend love fests and Israeli-style jaunts; of celebrities who gave concerts for his campaigns and never received thank-you notes or even his full attention during the performance; of public servants upset because they knocked themselves out at the president's request and never got a pat on the back; of V.I.P.'s disappointed to get pictures of themselves with the president with the customary signature withheld; of politicians disaffected by the president's penchant for not letting members of Congress or local pols stand on stage with him when he's speaking in their state (they often watch from the audience and sometimes have to lobby just to get a shout-out); of power brokers, local and national, who felt that the president insulted them by never seeking their advice or asking them to come to the White House or ride along in the limo for a schmooze.

10   Care and feeding has been outsourced to Joe Biden, who loves it, but it doesn't build the same kind of loyalty as when the president does it.

11   ③ <u>"He comes from the neediest profession of all, except for acting, but he is not needy and he doesn't fully understand the neediness of others; it's an abstraction to him," says Jonathan Alter, who wrote "The Promise" about Obama's first year in office and is working on a sequel. "He's not an ungracious person, but he can be guilty of ingratitude. It's not a politically smart way for him to operate."</u>

12   Newman wanted to be an actor, not a movie star. Obama wants to be a policy maker, not a glad-handing pol. Sometimes after political events, even small meetings, he requires decompression time. Unlike Harry Truman or George Bush senior, he prefers not to mix relaxing with networking. He sticks mostly to golf with his male aides.

13   "Needy politicians, like Bill Clinton, recharge at political events," says Alter. "But, for Obama, they deplete rather than create energy."

14   ④ Richard Wolffe, the author of Obama portraits, "Renegade" and "Revival," agreed: "The very source of his strength as an individual, that he willed himself into being, that he's a solitary figure who doesn't need many people, is also clearly a weakness. There are people who've worked with him for years who don't understand why he gives so little back."

15   From the first time Obama made a splash with an anti-apartheid speech at Occidental College, says David Maraniss, author of "Barack Obama: The Story," he has been ambivalent, even perverse.

16   "He realized that he could stir crowds while also thinking to himself that it was all a game and posturing," the biographer said. "He is always removed and participating at the same time, self-conscious and without the visceral need or love of transactional politics that would characterize Bill Clinton or L. B. J. or even W., in a way."

17   ⑤ What will save him, Maraniss believes, is his fierce competitive will. "His is cool and Clinton's is hot, but they burn at the same temperature inside," he said. "So he does some of what he finds distasteful, but not all of it, and not all of it very well."

18   One thing, though: Paul Newman sent thank-you notes.

(From *The New York Times*, August 8, 2012)

Notes

[1] **Maureen Bridgid Dowd**: Born on January 14, 1952, is an American columnist for *The New York Times* and best-selling author. During the 1970s and the early 1980s, she worked for *Time* magazine and *the Washington Star*, where she covered news as well as sports and wrote feature articles. Dowd joined *the Times* in 1983 as a metropolitan reporter and eventually became an Op-Ed writer for the newspaper in 1995. In 1999, she was awarded a Pulitzer Prize for her series of columns on the Monica Lewinsky scandal in the Clinton administration.

[2] **Paul Leonard Newman** (1925 – 2008): An American actor, film director, entrepreneur, professional racing driver and team owner; he was also an environmentalist, liberal social activist and philanthropist. He won numerous awards, including an Academy Award for his performance in the 1986 film *The Color of Money*, a BAFTA Award, a Screen Actors Guild Award, a Cannes Film Festival Award, an Emmy Award, and many honorary awards. He also won several national championships as a driver in Sports Car Club of America road racing, and his race teams won several championships in open wheel IndyCar racing.

Words and Phrases

estate /ɪˈsteɪt/ *n.*

a large area of land, usually in the country, that is owned by one person or family 庄园

shimmer /ˈʃɪmə(r)/ *v.*

to shine with a soft light that seems to move slightly 闪烁

dahlia /ˈdeɪliə/ *n.*

a large brightly coloured garden flower, often shaped like a ball 大丽花属

aloof /əˈluːf/ *adj.*
  not friendly or interested in other people 冷漠的
wary /ˈweərɪ/ *adj.*
  careful when dealing with sb./sth. because you think that there may be a danger or problem 谨慎的
cuddly /ˈkʌdli/ *adj.*
  inviting cuddling or hugging 令人想拥抱的
dysfunction /dɪsˈfʌŋkʃn/ *n.*
  a failure to work well 功能障碍
self-made /ˈselfˈmeɪd/ *adj.*
  having become rich and successful through your own hard work rather than having had money given to you 白手起家的
brash /bræʃ/ *adj.*
  confident in an aggressive way 盛气凌人的
upend /ʌpˈend/ *v.*
  to turn sb./sth. upside down 使颠倒
Shaker /ˈʃeɪkə(r)/ *n.*
  a member of a religious group in the U.S. who live in a community in a very simple way and do not marry or have partners 震颤派教徒
aesthetic /iːsˈθetɪk/ *n.*
  the aesthetic qualities and ideas of sth. 审美观
rococo /rəˈkəʊkəʊ/ *adj.*
  ornate or florid 过分修饰的
moneybags /ˈmʌnɪbægz/ *n.*
  a very rich person 阔佬
fest /fest/ *n.*
  a festival or large meeting involving a particular activity or with a particular atmosphere 大型聚会
jaunt /dʒɔːnt/ *n.*
  a short journey that you make for pleasure 旅行

withhold /'wɪð'həʊld/ v.

to refuse to give sth. to sb. 不给

disaffected /ˌdɪsə'fektɪd/ adj.

no longer satisfied with your situation, organization, belief etc. and therefore not loyal to it 不满的

penchant /'pentʃənt/ n.

a special liking for sth. 爱好

schmooze /ʃmuːz/ n.

a chat 闲聊

glad-hand /'glædhænd/ v.

to say hello to sb. in a friendly way, especially when this is not sincere 热情地打招呼

decompression /ˌdiːkəm'preʃn/ n.

the act of or process of allowing sth. that has been compressed to fill the space that it originally took up 解压缩

anti-apartheid /'æntɪə'pɑːtheɪt/ adj.

opposed to apartheid 反种族隔离的

posturing /'pɒstʃərɪŋ/ n.

behaviour that is not natural or sincere but is intended to attract attention or to have a particular effect 做作的举止

visceral /'vɪsərəl/ adj.

resulting from strong feelings rather than careful thought 出自内心的

distasteful /dɪs'teɪstfl/ adj.

unpleasant or offensive 使人不愉快的

make a splash

to do sth. in a way that attracts a lot of attention or causes a lot of excitement 引起轰动

Reading Comprehension Questions

1. In the opinion of Harvey Weinstein, Barack Obama is _____.

    (A) wary (B) unpopular

    (C) inconsiderate (D) like Paul Newman

2. The word "beholden" in paragraph 5 most probably means _____.

    (A) owing thanks (B) duty bound

    (C) sensitive (D) attentive

3. Who describes Obama as a self-made president?

    (A) Paul Newman. (B) The author.

    (C) Jonathan Alter. (D) Richard Wolffe.

4. We can learn from the text that _____.

    (A) Bill Clinton gave little back as a president

    (B) Harry Truman rarely mixed relaxing with networking

    (C) Joe Biden is a more successful politician than Barack Obama

    (D) Barack Obama's treatment of his supporters is unfavorable to him

5. According to David Maraniss, which of the following is favorable to Obama? _____

    (A) His fierce competitive will. (B) His ambivalence.

    (C) His selective insensitivity. (D) His ingratitude.

(选文、注释:任爱军)

2. The Five Images of Love

By Grace Rhys[1]

1 ① No one understands the nature of love; it is like a bird of heaven that sings a strange language. It lights down among us, coming from whence we know not, going we know not how or when, striking out wild notes of music that make even fatigued and heavy hearts to throb and give back a tone of courage.

2 The sorts and kinds of love are infinite in number, infinite as the days of the years of time. Each one of us is capable of many and various loves. We cannot love two creatures, not two dogs, with the same love. To each of those whom we love we offer a gem of different colour and value; to the unknown Master of the heavens, ah! who shall tell of what sort is the love we offer to Him? Yet in this love, too (which is natural worship), we discover the same vibrational atmosphere that invades the soul of all lovers.

3 ② I doubt we shall not get much nearer to the nature of love by mere talking. Intellectual statements are of little use. God does not make intellectual statements, He creates. We have to find our way about in the vast medley of created things that life spreads out around us, and pick up what bits of knowledge we can as we make our way along.

4 Let me choose five images that will give an idea of what the awaking of this new life means.

5 Ⅰ. Shall we not say that the creature without love is like the lamp unlit? There it is, and no one needs it. But touch it with flame, and it trembles and glows and becomes the centre of the room where it stands. Everything that falls under its rays is new-gilt. So does the lover see all natural things quite new.

6 Ⅱ. Or take the image of the withering plant that is dying of drought. The

sun's rays have parched it; the roots have searched and searched for moisture in a soil that grows every day harder and drier. The plant wilts and hangs its head; it is fainting and ready to die, when down comes the rain in a murmuring multitude of round scented drops, the purest thing alive, a distilled essence, necessary to life. Under that baptism the plant lifts itself up; it drinks and rejoices. In the night it renews its strength; in the morning the heat it has had from the sun, reinforced by the rain, bursts out into coloured flowers. ③ So I have known a man battered by hard life and the excess of his own passions: I have seen love come to such a man and take him up and cleanse him and set him on his feet; and from him has burst forth a flood of colour and splendour—creative work that now lends its fiery stimulus to thousands.

7   Ⅲ. Another image might be of the harp that stands by itself in golden aloofness. Then come the beautiful arms, the curving fingers that pluck at the strings, and the air is filled with melody; the harp begins to live, thrilling and rejoicing, down to its golden foot.

8   Ⅳ. Or picture the unlighted house, empty at fall of night. The windows are dark; the door shut; the clean wind goes about and about it, and cannot find an entrance. The dull heavy air is faint within; it longs to be reunited to the wind of the world outside. Then comes the woman with the key, and in she steps; the windows are opened, the imprisoned air rushes out, the wind enters; the lamps and the fire are lit; so that light fills windows and doors. The tables are set, there is the sound of footsteps; and more footsteps. The house glows and lives.

9   One could please oneself by many more images; such as the white garment of feathers that the young swans put on in the spring: the young flowers opening out their cups to the Sun that fills them with his golden wine. All life is full of such images, because nature has ruled that love, energy, beauty, and joy are one.

10   Ⅴ. A last image only I would like to add because of the pleasure it has given me. On the north door of the Cathedral of Chartres[2] there is a

sculptured design, some six hundred years old, of God creating the birds. God is charming, quite young, not more than thirty-eight or so; He has a most sweet expression. Behind Him a little stands the Son, about seventeen, tall as He and very like Him, but beardless. He has the same sweetness of look, as though upon each countenance an ineffable smile were just dawning. The Father is holding something that time has broken in His hand; most likely it is a bird. What a fortunate moment! What a fortunate thought! No wonder they both look pleased. Never have the birds disappointed Him as have we, His ruder children. Every spring since then these small creatures praise Him, head turned skywards, for the joy of the beloved, for the secret nest.

11 ④ Imagining and pondering, one is apt to grow a little wise; now perhaps we may say that love is a radiant atmosphere of the soul, a celestial energy, a fluid force.

12 This force, this energy is set running in the wide kingdom that is within us by some Spirit touch. A soft tumult takes place in the life within; waves on waves of joy, desire, grief, ecstasy begin to run, making a trembling music that often causes the whole body to shake and tremble too.

13 ⑤ I am in love with love; I do adore it; — from the smile on that rough fellow's face as he talks to his dog, to the ardours of a St. Francis[3] or a Joan of Arc[4]. That bright creative flame, winged, conferring the gift of tongues, master of all music, of all joy, is the best thing we have of life.

(From *Modern English Essays*, New York: Dutton & Co. 1922:174)

Notes

[1] **Grace Rhys** (*née* Little, 1865 – 1929): An Irish writer brought up in Boyle, County Roscommon. Joseph Bennet Little, her landowner father, lost his money through gambling and, after receiving a good education from governesses, she and her sisters had to move to London as adults to earn a

living. She was both wife and literary companion to Ernest Percival Rhys whom she met at a garden party given by Yeats. They married in 1891 and sometimes worked side by side in the British Museum. Her first novel, *Mary Dominic*, was published in 1898. Several of her stories have an Irish setting, including *The Charming of Estercel* (1904) set in Elizabethan Ireland, which was illustrated by Howard Pyle in Harper's Magazine. Her other work includes *The Wooing of Sheila* (1901), *The Bride* (1909), and *Five Beads on a String* (1907), a book of essays. She also wrote poetry and books for children, and had a son and two daughters of her own. The Rhys were known for entertaining writers and critics at their London home on Sunday afternoons. Grace died in Washington while accompanying her husband on an American lecture tour.

[2] **The Cathedral of Chartres**: Also called Notre-Dame d'Chartres or the Cathedral of Notre-Dame, Gothic cathedral located in the town of Chartres, northwestern France. Generally ranked as one of the three chief examples of Gothic French architecture (along with Amiens Cathedral and Reims Cathedral), it is noted not only for its architectural innovations but also for its numerous sculptures and its much-celebrated stained glass. The cathedral's association with the Virgin Mary (the supposed veil of the Virgin is kept in the cathedral treasury) made it the destination of pilgrims in the Middle Ages.

[3] **St. Francis** (1182 – 1226): An Italian religious leader and Catholic mystic who founded the Order of Friars Minor, more commonly known as the Franciscans. He is known as the patron saint of animals, birds, and the environment. Though baptized as Giovanni Bernardone he was commonly known as Francesco.

[4] **Joan of Arc** (1412 – 1431): Nicknamed "The Maid of Orléans", is considered a heroine of France for her role during the Lancastrian phase of the Hundred Years' War, and was canonized as a Roman Catholic saint. Joan of Arc was born to Jacques d'Arc and Isabelle, a peasant family, at Domrémy in north-east France. Joan said she received visions of the Archangel Michael, Saint Margaret, and Saint Catherine instructing her to support Charles Ⅶ and

recover France from English domination late in the Hundred Years' War. The uncrowned King Charles Ⅶ sent Joan to the siege of Orléans as part of a relief mission. She gained prominence after the siege was lifted only nine days later. Several additional swift victories led to Charles Ⅶ's coronation at Reims. This long-awaited event boosted French morale and paved the way for the final French victory. On May 23 1430, she was captured at Compiègne by the Burgundian faction which was allied with the English. She was later handed over to the English, and then put on trial by the pro-English Bishop of Beauvais Pierre Cauchon on a variety of charges. After Cauchon declared her guilty she was burned at the stake on May 30 1431, dying at about nineteen years of age. Twenty-five years after her execution, an inquisitorial court authorized by Pope Callixtus Ⅲ examined the trial, debunked the charges against her, pronounced her innocent, and declared her a martyr. In the 16th century she became a symbol of the Catholic League, and in 1803 she was declared a national symbol of France by the decision of Napoleon Bonaparte. She was beatified in 1909 and canonized in 1920. Joan of Arc is one of the nine secondary patron saints of France, along with St. Denis, St. Martin of Tours, St. Louis, St. Michael, St. Remi, St. Petronilla, St. Radegund and St. Thérèse of Lisieux. Joan of Arc has remained a popular figure in literature, painting, sculpture, and other cultural works since the time of her death, and many famous writers, filmmakers and composers have created works about her. Cultural depictions of her have continued in films, theater, television, video games, music, and performances to this day.

Words and Phrases

fatigued /fəˈtiːgd/ *adj.*

    very tired, both physically and mentally　精疲力竭的；身心交瘁的

throb /θrɒb/ *v.*

    to beat or sound with a strong, regular rhythm　跳动；搏动

gem /dʒem/ *n.*

(gemstone) a precious stone that has been cut and polished and is used in jewellery 宝石

wither /ˈwɪðə(r)/ *v.*

wither (sth.) if a plant withers or something withers it, it dries up and dies 枯萎；凋谢

parch /pɑːtʃ/ *v.*

(especially of hot weather) to make an area of land very dry 使（土地）极其干燥

wilt /wɪlt/ *v.*

to droop or shrivel through lack of water, too much heat, or disease, or make a plant droop or shrivel 枯萎；衰弱

murmuring /ˈmɜːmərɪŋ/ *n.*

a low or indistinct continuous sound 低沉的声音

multitude /ˈmʌltɪtjuːd/ *n.*

(of sth./sb.) an extremely large number of things or people 众多；大量

distil /dɪˈstɪl/ *v.*

sth. (from/into sth.) (formal) to get the essential meaning or ideas from thoughts, information, experiences, etc. 吸取精华；提炼

rejoice /rɪˈdʒɔɪs/ *v.*

to express great happiness about something 非常高兴；深感欣喜

batter /ˈbætə(r)/ *v.*

to hit sb./sth. hard many times, especially in a way that causes serious damage 连续猛击

splendour /ˈsplendə(r)/ *n.*

grand and impressive beauty 壮丽；华丽

fiery /ˈfaɪəri/ *adj.*

looking like fire; consisting of fire 火一般的

stimulus /ˈstɪmjələs/ *n.*

that helps sb./sth. to develop better or more quickly 激励因素；促进因素

harp /hɑːp/ n.

a large musical instrument with strings stretched on a vertical frame, played with the fingers 竖琴

melody /ˈmelədi/ n.

a tune, especially the main tune in a piece of music written for several instruments or voices 旋律

imprisoned /ɪmˈprɪznd/ adj.

kept in prison; captive 被囚禁的

garment /ˈɡɑːmənt/ n.

a piece of clothing 衣服

countenance /ˈkaʊntənəns/ n.

a person's face or their expression 面容；面部表情

ponder /ˈpɒndə(r)/ v.

to think about sth. carefully for a period of time 沉思；考虑

celestial /səˈlestiəl/ adj.

of the sky or of heaven 天上的

tumult /ˈtjuːmʌlt/ n.

a confused situation in which there is usually a lot of noise and excitement, often involving large numbers of people 喧哗；混乱

ecstasy /ˈekstəsi/ n.

a feeling or state of very great happiness 狂喜；陶醉；入迷

ardour /ˈɑːdə/ n.

very strong feelings of enthusiasm or love 激情；热情

confer /kənˈfɜː(r)/ v.

(on/ about sth.) to discuss something with somebody, in order to exchange opinions or get advice 商讨；交换意见

pick up

to get or obtain something 收集；得到

on one's feet

standing 站立

burst forth

to go or move somewhere suddenly with great force; to come from somewhere suddenly 突然出现,猛冲

pluck at

to play a musical instrument, especially a guitar, by pulling the strings with your fingers 拉

be apt to

likely or having a natural tendency to do something 易于……;有……倾向

Reading Comprehension Questions

1. The word "vibrational" in paragraph 2 is closest in meaning to _____.

    (A) rotational (B) oscillatory

    (C) pivoted   (D) rotating

2. According to the text, which of the following is NOT correct? _____

    (A) The sorts and kinds of love are immense in number.

    (B) We can give different creatures the same love.

    (C) Everyone is capable of many and various kinds of loves.

    (D) We offer to God the love that invades the soul of all lovers.

3. The main point of paragraph 3 is _____.

    (A) The author believes that through talking we can get to the nature of love

    (B) God creates intellectual statements

    (C) Only by finding our own way and picking up knowledge can we make our way to get nearer to the nature of love

    (D) The vast combination of created things can help us get much nearer to the nature of love

4. Which image does NOT belong to the five images the author mentioned?

(A) the withering plant that is dying of drought.

(B) the harp that stands by itself in golden aloofness.

(C) the unlighted house, empty at fall of night.

(D) the white garment of feathers that the young swans put on in the spring.

5. The last image of love belongs to _____.

(A) brotherhood

(B) family love

(C) love between parents and children

(D) love felt from religion

(选文、注释:何朝阳)

3. Embracing the Mystery of Einstein

Rhonda Talbot[1]

The writer finds inspiration in the legendary scientist's words and life lessons.

1 When I was eight years old, my mother handed me a slip of paper with an Einstein quote: ① "He who joyfully marches to music in rank and file has already earned my contempt. He has been given a large brain by mistake, since for him the spinal cord[2] would surely suffice."

2 Why she gave this to me and not her other five children remains unclear. Perhaps she saw my disillusionment with the rat-a-tat, airless echo of school, the Catholic Church, the Sunday roast dinners and our predictable life. I had been punished a number of times for staring out the school window daydreaming about who knows what, maybe stink bugs. Then came the thwack of the ruler, held by a tight-fisted, chalky nun who sent me off to kneel on the concrete hallway floor for two hours. I would later go home and draw pictures of nuns being kidnapped, held in dark closets, being starved, begging for mercy. I hid the stories under my bed, accompanying the other stacks, all concerning some level of inequality.

3 During this time, music and freedom called my mother to another place, a more hopeful existence where she wouldn't be a "wife". She was a hippy to my father's buttoned-up businessman. My mother did not have many heroes, as they were fleeting and then dead: Malcolm X, Martin Luther King Jr. and the Kennedys. But there was something about Einstein that settled into her very core, then mine.

A New Life Began and I Took Albert Along As a Companion

4 In 1969, she had had enough. She confided in me: "We are leaving. Tell no one; your sisters won't understand. Your father will return to an empty house, to complement his empty existence."

5 Then: "Imagination is more important than knowledge. Don't forget that. Ever."

6 Thus began my own obsession with Einstein. I tucked these quotes into my grandmother's jewelry box, which she had given me just prior to her death.

7 ② Legions of people remain enamored by this brilliant man, not just for what he discovered, accomplished and how he radically changed the world, but because of his childlike innocence, his unlimited curiosity, great humility, a legacy of words that continue to endure. When you ask a complete stranger who defines genius, they might reply, "Oh, Einstein."

8 And he was a rascal, with wild eyes, the mop of hair, his crumpled clothes. This made him real for the rest of us. I began to collect quotes and read about him in libraries. His humor brought me great comfort. He wasn't some impervious man one couldn't access. He didn't believe in separating himself from others, and in fact loved sharing his ideas, while helping others expand on their own. He was approachable, both alive and dead.

9 Born with a kind of eternal intelligence, his curiosity about all things began to emerge at age four. While examining his father's pocket compass, Einstein was baffled. What was causing the needle to move? The empty space made no sense to him. He began to build models and mechanical devices for fun. He wanted answers. Age 10, he met Max Talmey, a poor, Jewish medical student from Poland, who introduced him to science, math, philosophy, Immanuel Kant's Critique of Pure Reason and Euclid's Elements, which Einstein dubbed "the holy little geometry book".

He Was Brilliant in His Own Way

10   As a boy, his father knew little Albert was gifted, and perhaps because the elder Einstein (an engineer) had failed at so many businesses, he insisted his son stay in school. He enrolled him in a school in Munich to pursue engineering, but Albert was frustrated with the educational system. He clashed repeatedly with the authorities, resented their teaching style and wrote about how schools were essentially killing the creative spirit and curiosity of its students. He was 15.

11   "The only thing that interferes with my learning is my education." When I read this in junior high school, I could finally relax. The simple statement brought along a universe of vindication because I simply could not understand the entire educational process of rote learning. It was too boxed in, too impersonal. I realized I would have to find my own way intellectually alongside the traditional, through books and lectures by Rollo May, Erich Fromm, B.F. Skinner, Timothy Leary and Marshall McLuhan.

12   I was no genius, simply curious and bored with school. Given the number of times my gypsy mother moved us, staying on track in class made me weary. Another school, another teacher, another set of young people I would have to navigate somehow.

13   Why has Einstein resonated so deeply with me and so many others? Among the world's most brilliant minds, he continues to inspire. What of Leonardo da Vinci[3], Nikola Tesla[4], Newton, Hawking, Aristotle, Edison, Miguel de Cervantes[5]? The list goes on. They too share not just powerful minds, but an endless pursuit through curiosity and instinct. They knew knowledge was important, had to be learned, but could only get them so far. The rest is mystery.

14   ③ Einstein embodies the mystery. So many of his ideas, beyond his incredible discoveries in the world itself, which ultimately turned the world on its head, contain room, empty space, air to breathe. His equation, $E = mc^2$,

may be the most famous equation in physics, eventually setting the stage for the development of the atomic bomb and nuclear power plants. But had he known where this was going, he said, he should have become a watchmaker.

15   To this day, his theories inspire advances in science, astronomy and physics, as well as from philosophers. I keep a tip sheet of quotes tacked up near my computer and read one every day. It really doesn't matter which one, as they all carry great meaning. With each read I come away with yet another interpretation.

16   Einstein would go on to fail countless exams when applying to higher learning institutions. Yet, he continued exploring, reading and taking great interest in other's concepts and ideas. He did eventually get accepted into the Polytechnic in Zurich. He wanted more knowledge and continued developing his own theories and expanding others.

His Instincts Propelled Him Yet Further

17   He never lost his ability to stay curious, intuitive and of course, humorous. Despite his apparent genius, upon graduation he could not get a job and landed at the patent office, only to be overlooked for a promotion because he had not managed to grasp machine technology. But it was there that the 26-year-old developed further radical notions in his spare time by analyzing various patents. And he never stopped writing about his findings.

18   Finally, with some recognition, he left the patent office, and by 1908 was considered as one of the world's leading scientists. He went on to become a professor in Prague and Berlin, and ultimately became famous a few years later when his theory of relativity at last made a permanent impression on the world. Ten years later, he was awarded the Nobel Prize in Physics.

19   For many years later, he traveled the globe. He maintained his own humility until the day he died. He was a genius, but also a gentleman, a humorist, altruist, artist and a great believer in love. "How on earth are you ever going to explain in terms of chemistry and physics so important a biological

phenomenon as first love?"

20 The entire universe was Einstein's canvas, and he made this world relatable to all of us. I've been to my fair share of enlightenment lectures, often given by physicists turned "gurus," and there they sit, spouting what I had already learned by Einstein's words:

21 ④ "Anyone who has never made a mistake has never tried anything new."

22 "Great spirits have often encountered violent opposition from weak minds."

23 "We can't solve problems by using the same kind of thinking we used when we created them."

24 And of course, perhaps the most famous, his definition of insanity: "Doing the same thing over and over again and expecting different results."

Meanwhile, Back in New Jersey

25 Of all the great brains, his would be the one cut into 240 pieces, kept in jars, cardboard boxes, often hidden, studied under microscopes. Bits of his grey matter still remain at Princeton University. All those years of cutting, probing and analyzing amounted to little new knowledge of the human mind.

26 ⑤ The contradiction rattles the very jars into a pulpy mess, if only because it contradicts what Einstein tried to impress. Stay curious and questioning; love the mystery. Conventional knowledge, though essential, is finite. Imagination is not. This is what Einstein embraced. Perhaps the lore of his brain in a jar helps prolong the iconic myth. In his words: "The most beautiful thing we can experience is the mysterious. It is the source of all true art and all science. He to whom this emotion is a stranger, who can no longer pause to wonder and strand rapt in awe, is as good as dead: his eyes are closed."

27 Recently, while driving my own eight-year-old girls to school, I said, "Remember, imagination is more important than knowledge."

28   Through the rear view mirror, I watched them both roll their eyes in that "Please mom, just drive," kind of way, as they said in unison, "OK, Einstein."

(From *The Spring* 2013 *issue of Positive Magazine*)

Notes

[1] **Rhonda Talbot**: A Los Angeles based author, screenwriter and film executive. Her stories and essays can be seen in *The Los Angeles Times*, *More Magazine*, *Salon*, *Oddville Press*, *The Rusty Nail*, *Thought Catalogue*, *Cultural Weekly*, among others.

[2] **The Spinal Cord**: The cylindrical bundle of nerve fibres and associated tissue which is enclosed in the spine and connects nearly all parts of the body to the brain, with which it forms the central nervous system.

[3] **Leonardo da Vinci** (1452 – 1519): An Italian painter, scientist, and engineer.

[4] **Nikola Tesla** (1856 – 1943): American electrical engineer and inventor who developed the first alternating-current induction motor, as well as several forms of oscillators, the Tesla coil, and a wireless guidance system for ships.

[5] **Miguel de Cervantes** (1547 – 1616): A Spanish novelist and dramatist whose most famous work is *Don Quixote* (1605 – 1615), a satire on chivalric romances that greatly influenced the development of the novel.

Words and Phrases

disillusionment /ˌdɪsɪˈluːʒnmənt/ *n*.

a feeling of disappointment resulting from the discovery that something is not as good as one believed it to be 理想破灭

rat-tat (also **rat-a-tat**) /ˌrætəˈtæt/ *n*.

a rapping sound (used especially in reference to a sequence of knocks on a door or the sound of gunfire) 砰砰敲门声

suffice /sə'faɪs/ v.

be enough or adequate 足够

thwack /θwæk/ n.

a sharp blow 重击

fleeting /'fliːtɪŋ/ adj.

lasting for a very short time 短暂的

obsession /əb'seʃn/ n.

the state of being obsessed with someone or something 痴迷

rascal /'rɑːskl/ n.

a mischievous or cheeky person, especially a child or man (typically used in an affectionate way 开玩笑的说法;淘气的人(尤指小孩)

impervious /ɪm'pɜːviəs/ adj.

unable to be affected or influenced by 不受影响的

eternal /ɪ'tɜːnl/ adj.

used to emphasize expressions of admiration, gratitude, etc. 永恒的

dub /dʌb/ v.

give an unofficial name or nickname to 起绰号

propel /prə'pel/ v.

drive or push something forwards 驱动

radical /'rædɪkl/ adj.

(especially of change or action) relating to or affecting the fundamental nature of something; far-reaching or thorough 根本的

humility /hju'mɪlɪtɪ/ n.

the quality or state of being humble 谦卑

confide in

trust (someone) enough to tell them of a secret or private matter 信任

a legion/legions of

a vast number of people or things 众多

interfere with

prevent (a process or activity) from continuing or being carried out properly 妨碍

be enamored by

have a liking or admiration for 迷恋

set the stage for

prepare the conditions for (the occurrence or beginning of something) 为……打好基础,为……创造条件

expand on

give a fuller version or account of 详述

Suggested Topics for Writing

1. Einstein's teachers in Germany didn't like him because he asked too many questions. Einstein's family is very special: they discussed a lot with Albert about things he liked and never criticized him. Do you agree or disagree with the following statement? Parents are a more important influence than teachers on a child's success in school. Use specific reasons and examples to support your answer.

2. In your opinion, what is the most important characteristic (for example, intelligence, honesty, a sense of humor) that a person can have to be successful in life? Use specific reasons and examples from your experience to explain your answer.

(选文、注释:斯骏)

Unit Fourteen   New Horizon

1. What If Women Ruled the World?

By Dee Dee Myers[1]

Not so long ago, the idea that women might rule the world seemed slightly ridiculous — like something out of science fiction. But in an essay to mark International Women's Day, political analyst and former White House press secretary Dee Dee Myers argues it's now a topic that can be seriously discussed.

1   ① <u>Women clearly lacked the intellectual capacity and emotional fortitude to make the difficult decisions that leadership required. It wasn't bias, it was biology — it was just the way women were made.</u>

2   But that was then. In recent decades, attitudes and ideas have changed — and fast. That's not to say that every corner of the world has welcomed women moving from the traditional and private into the modern and public. But move they have.

3   So what's changed? A lot. As a huge and growing body of research and experience makes clear, empowering women makes things better. Not perfect. But better.

4   Business is more profitable. Governments are more representative. Families are stronger, and communities are healthier. There is less violence — and more peace, stability and sustainability.

5   Why? Well, it starts with the simple fact that women often experience life differently. And that experience affects the way we see problems — and think about solutions.

6   "Diversity is absolutely an asset," says Christine Lagarde[2], the managing director of the International Monetary Fund[3].

7   ② "With diversity you bring different ways of looking at the world, different ways of analysing issues, different ways of offering solutions. The sheer fact of diversity actually increases the horizon and enriches the thinking process, which is critical."

8   Both women and men often say that women communicate differently, that they listen, encourage dialogue, and build consensus.

9   Studies also show that women also lead differently than men. They're more likely to be collaborative, inclusive and team-oriented, all characteristics that tend to be effective, particularly in today's less-hierarchical, fast-paced, innovation-driven world.

10   "I think it's fair to say that women are a little more collaborative in their approach overall, and a little less driven to conflict as opposed to driven to working out problems," says Janet Napolitano, the U. S. Secretary of Homeland Security[4].

11   Mary Robinson, the former president of Ireland, says that women also bring an inter-generational perspective to their work. "We need to take decisions now that will make for a safer world for our grandchildren and their grandchildren, and I think women are more likely to do that when they come into positions of leadership."

12   Acknowledging that men and women bring different qualities and different skills to public life is critical. For too long, women were expected to think like men and act like men if they wanted to succeed.

13   But increasingly their differences are seen as a source of strength rather than a weakness to be overcome.

14   Nancy Pelosi, the first woman to serve as Speaker of the U. S. House of

Representatives[5], tells women to simply be themselves. "You are the only person who can make your unique contribution. Your authenticity is your strength, be you."

15 ③ That's not to say there aren't obstacles, there are. Women have long been judged by a double standard. Study after study shows that their accomplishments are just a little less valued — and they have less margin for error.

16 Sometimes it's women who hold themselves back - they don't own their own value, raise their hands for promotions or ask for more money.

17 Despite these ongoing challenges, the benefits of empowering women are undeniable. Women are the engine driving global economic growth.

18 Last year, women were responsible for \$20tn (£13.3tn) in spending, and by 2014, that number is expected to increase to \$28tn (£18.6tn). And when women have more cash, they spend it differently. They feed their families healthier diets and send their children to school. They invest in clean water, better schools, education and health care. They start businesses and hire other women. The entire community prospers.

19 As a result, investing in women has become more than good public relations. It has become a strategic imperative for companies around the world.

20 Women are also essential to building and sustaining peace. Today, nearly half of peace agreements fail within five years in no small measure because half the stakeholders are excluded.

21 ④ When women are at the table, they help bridge the gap between different groups and ensure that a broader range of issues, from food security to sexual violence, are addressed. As a result, peace is more likely to take root.

22 Former U.S. Secretary of State Dr. Condoleezza Rice[6] says she has learned first-hand that you need women to participate in the peace process.

23 "First and foremost women are often the guardians of the village, the family, and are therefore the ones who suffer most in conflict zones. They're often the target of marauding forces, the target of those who would rape and

maim and if you can engage them in the process, then they also can help the society to heal."

24 ⑤ <u>So empowering women isn't about political correctness, it's about improving outcomes. It's about investing in stronger economies and healthier communities — it's about ending conflicts, and sustaining peace. It's about improving the quality of life for people all over the world.</u>

25 Empowering women isn't just the right thing, it's the necessary thing. And because women are increasingly ruling, the world is changing for the better.

(From BBC, March 8, 2013)

Notes

[1] **Dee Dee Myers**: Margaret Jane "Dee Dee" Myers was born on September 1, 1961, a political analyst, was the White House Press Secretary during the first two years of the Clinton administration, from January 1993 to December 1994. She was the first woman and the second-youngest person to hold that position.

[2] **Christine Lagarde**: Christine Madeleine Odette Lagarde was born on 1 January 1956, is a French lawyer and politician who has been the Managing Director (MD) of the International Monetary Fund (IMF) since July 5, 2011.

[3] **The International Monetary Fund (IMF)**: It is an international organization headquartered in Washington, D.C., of 189 countries working to foster global monetary cooperation, secure financial stability, facilitate international trade, promote high employment and sustainable economic growth, and reduce poverty around the world. Formed in 1944 at the Bretton Woods Conference, it came into formal existence in 1945 with 29 member countries and the goal of reconstructing the international payment system.

[4] **Homeland Security**: It is an American umbrella term for "the national

effort to ensure a homeland that is safe, secure, and resilient against terrorism and other hazards where American interests, aspirations, and ways of life can thrive to the national effort to prevent terrorist attacks within the United States, reduce the vulnerability of the U.S. to terrorism, and minimize the damage from attacks that do occur.

[5] **Speaker of the U.S. House of Representatives**: Also called the Speaker of the House, the presiding officer of the United States House of Representatives.

[6] **Condoleezza Rice**: Born on November 14, 1954, is an American political scientist and diplomat. She served as the 66th United States Secretary of State, the second person to hold that office in the administration of President George W. Bush. Rice was the first female African-American Secretary of State, as well as the second African-American Secretary of State after Colin Powell.

Words and Phrases

fortitude /ˈfɔːtɪtjuːd/ *n.*

courage shown by sb. who is suffering great pain or facing great difficulties 刚毅

sustainability /səsteɪnəˈbɪlɪti/ *n.*

the ability to maintain the desirable state 持续性

asset /ˈæset/ *n.*

a person or thing that is valuable or useful 有价值的人或物

sheer /ʃɪə(r)/ *adj.*

complete and not mixed with anything else 完全的;纯粹的

consensus /kənˈsensəs/ *n.*

an opinion that all members of a group agree with 共识

hierarchical /ˌhaɪəˈrɑːkɪkl/ *adj.*

arranged in a system, in which people are organized into different levels of importance from highest to lowest 等级制度的

authenticity   /ˌɔːθenˈtɪsəti/   n.

the quality of being genuine or true 真实性；确实性

own   /əʊn/   v.

to acknowledge or admit something 承认

imperative   /ɪmˈperətɪv/   n.

something that must be done 必须做的事

stakeholder   /ˈsteɪkhəʊldə(r)/   n.

a person or group with a direct interest, involvement, or investment in something 利益攸关方

maraud   /məˈrɔːd/   v.

raid for plunder 抢劫

maim   /meɪm/   v.

to injure sb. seriously, causing permanent damage to their body 使残废；使受重伤

outcome   /ˈaʊtkʌm/   n.

the way that something turns out in the end 结果

hold back

to keep back or restrain somebody from doing something 阻止；抑制

take root

to become established and accepted 生根；扎根

Reading Comprehension Questions

1. Compared with men, women were believed to be _____.

    (A) able to make business more profitable

    (B) less biased in governing a country

    (C) biologically inferior in making critical decisions

(D) moving faster into the modern and public

2. According to Christine Lagarde, women have the advantage that _____.

   (A) their view of the world is broader

   (B) their assets are different

   (C) they communicate more effectively

   (D) they can make people agree with each other

3. The author believes that in today's less-hierarchical, fast-paced, innovation-driven world _____.

   (A) people are more inclusive and team-oriented

   (B) different opinions are valuable

   (C) the ability to analyse issues is vital

   (D) women are less opposed to working out problems

4. It used to be considered a disadvantage for women to _____.

   (A) consider about children and grandchildren

   (B) think like men and act like men in order to succeed

   (C) behave like themselves

   (D) have a double standard

5. One of the reasons to empower women is that _____.

   (A) they're often the target of marauding forces

   (B) the society will benefit as a whole

   (C) it can attract more investment

   (D) all peace agreements will be carried out smoothly

(选文、注释:徐守平)

2. The Soul of the Olympics

Frank Bruni[1]

1 It's easy to be cynical about the Olympics: about the runaway commercialism; about the jingoism that so many countries bring to the games; about NBC[2]. Definitely about NBC. Its breathless degree of fake suspense during prime time broadcasts has been a silly mockery of our wired ways, and too many on-the-spot interviews with athletes redefined dippy. How do you feel? Jubilant if you've medaled, crushed if you haven't and really, really tired. Fill in the blanks.

2 But you know what? It's just as easy to be sappy about the Olympics. In fact it's a whole lot easier. Because for all their flaws and frustrations, they've been a phenomenal spectacle. More than that, they've been a phenomenal inspiration, in precisely the ways that they were supposed to be, during a season when we needed the uplift. ① Amid bullets in Colorado and Wisconsin[3], vitriol on the campaign trail, ominously scorching heat and serious questions about whether we can and will rise to the challenges before us, the Olympics have affirmed that human potential is just about infinite and that the human soul is good. They've presented two solid weeks of parables, most of which underscored the great rewards possible when great risk is taken and the prospect of glory on the far side of sacrifice.

3 Gabby Douglas gave us a lesson in all of that. I can't quite let go of her smile or her story. Four years ago, at the age of 12, she unsuccessfully begged her mother, Natalie Hawkins, to allow her to leave their home in Virginia and train in Iowa, which seemed so distant and exotic that Hawkins once joked: "Are there people in Iowa? There's just corn."

4 Corn, that is, and a world-renowned coach who knows a thing or two

about harvesting Olympic gold. ② <u>Douglas joined forces with him when she was 14, and her mother finally consented to her wishes, placing her in the care of an Iowa family whom Douglas didn't yet know, in a town where a black girl was bound to stand out.</u> Many nights, Douglas has said, she cried herself to sleep. But she had this dream. And the only path to it, she felt certain, was through those cornfields.

5 The Olympics have reminded us that any grand achievement begins with a leap of faith and draws lavishly from a wellspring of pure confidence. And that what has been accomplished to date has no bearing on what can be accomplished in time.

6 ③ <u>The Dutch gymnast Epke Zonderland took to the air to prove as much, soaring above and swooping below the high bar during his gold-medal showstopper, while Michael Phelps took to the water. Before Phelps no man had won the same Olympic swimming event three times in a row. In London he did that. Before Phelps no man or woman had ever collected more than 18 Olympic medals. In London he did that, too. Then he collected a 20th, a 21st, a 22nd. All but four are gold. By multiple measures and by far, he is the most decorated Olympian ever.</u>

7 Mosts. Firsts. London brimmed with them, and they transcended mere trivia. They charted the march of social progress, marked the toppling of boundaries. For the first time, the American Olympic team had more women than men. For the first time, every national team included at least one woman, and that was because three Muslim countries that had never before sent a female athlete to the Olympics finally did so.

8 One of those countries was Saudi Arabia, and one of its two female competitors was Sarah Attar, who ran the 800 meters with her legs covered, her arms covered, her hair covered. At the start she beamed at the crowd, her smile an acknowledgment of history in the making. And though she lagged far behind everyone else in her heat, the crowd roared louder and louder as she approached the finish line, then gave her a standing ovation. It was as if she

had set a world record. Then again, she had.

9   ④ There was similar applause for Oscar Pistorius, the South African man who also challenged precedent and also defied limits, running the 400 meters on two prosthetic legs. He made it as far as the semifinals, after which the Grenadian runner Kirani James, who would go on to win the gold, swapped nametags with him. It was a gesture of the utmost respect and a poignant illustration of the kind of fellowship that athletic competition at its very best can foster.

10   For an illustration of the friendships it can forge, we had Misty May-Treanor and Kerri Walsh Jennings, who finished what they had decided would be their last Olympics together with a third consecutive gold in beach volleyball. At the net they were merciless. Away from it they were mush, taking tearful stock of their amazing adventure over the years and eloquently communicating just how much strength two people can wring from each other and how much support they can provide.

11   "I will never leave her side," May-Treanor, sitting next to Walsh Jennings, told Matt Lauer, adding that "that's what this Olympics signified — was the journey off the court together." Walsh Jennings, herself misty, put a hand on her friend's wrist. Medals are the least of what volleyball has given these two.

12   ⑤ From the Olympics we got validation that sports aren't just an engine of fame and a means to riches but a training ground for the rest of life, and that they can make champions proud without making them vain. Another smile I can't let go of is Missy Franklin's, toothy and triumphant, because I got the sense that the joy in it came not so much from besting her rivals in the pool but from meeting the grandest expectations that others had for her and that she had for herself.

13   As she won the first of four golds, in the 100-meter backstroke, NBC showed her high school classmates back in Colorado huddled in front of an enormous TV screen. They went bonkers when she touched the wall ahead of

everyone else. That reaction helped to explain a huge decision that she's made: rather than cash in on endorsement deals that could be worth hundreds of thousands, she'll preserve her amateur status so that she can swim for the team at whichever college she attends in the fall of 2013.

14   There will presumably be opportunities for money down the road. There won't be the same chance to bring excitement to her campus and play a special part on it. Those experiences can't be measured in dollars. And by choosing to savor them, she has something to teach us all.

(From *The New York Times*, August 11, 2012)

Notes

[1] **Frank Bruni** (1964 -   ): An American journalist. He was the chief restaurant critic of *The New York Times*, from 2004 to 2009. He is the author of two bestselling books, *Born Round*, a memoir about his family's love of food and his own struggles with overeating, and *Ambling into History*, about George W. Bush. The present article was taken from New York Times, August 11, 2012.

[2] **NBC**: Abbreviation for National Broadcasting Company in the U.S.

[3] **Bullets in Colorado and Wisconsin**: Referring to the two shootings in Colorado and Wisconsin in 2012. Shooting in Wisconsin took place at a Sikh temple in Oak Creek, on August 5. At least seven people were killed, including the suspected gunman. Colorado shooting: On July 20, 2012, a mass shooting occurred inside of a movie theater in Aurora, Colorado. A gunman shot into the audience with multiple firearms. 12 people were killed and 70 others were injured, the largest number of casualties in a shooting in the United States.

Words and Phrases

cynical   /ˈsɪnɪkl/   *adj.*

not believing that sth. good will happen or that sth. is important 怀疑的；愤世嫉俗的

jingoism /ˈdʒɪŋɡəʊɪzəm/ n.

a strong belief that your own country is best, especially when this is expressed in support of war with another country 极端爱国主义

jubilant /ˈdʒuːbɪlənt/ adj.

feeling or showing great happiness because of a success 喜气洋洋的；欢欣鼓舞的

vitriol /ˈvɪtrɪɒl/ n.

very cruel and bitter comments or criticism 尖酸刻薄的话或批评

ominously /ˈɒmənəsli/ adv.

in a way to suggest that sth. bad is going to happen in the future 带有不祥征兆地

parable /ˈpærəbl/ n.

a short story that teaches a moral or spiritual lesson, especially one of those told by Jesus as recorded in the *Bible* 尤指《圣经》中的寓言故事

swoop /swuːp/ v.

to fly quickly and suddenly downwards, especially in order to attack sb./sth. 向下猛冲；俯冲

brim /brɪm/ v.

to be full of sth. 盛满；充盈

transcend /trænˈsend/ v.

to be or go beyond the usual limits of sth. 超出；超越

trivia /ˈtrɪviə/ n.

unimportant matters, details or information 琐事；细枝末节

topple /ˈtɒpl/ v.

to become unsteady and fall down 倒塌

ovation /əʊˈveɪʃn/ n.

enthusiastic clapping by an audience as a sign of their approval 热烈鼓掌

prosthetic /prɒsˈθetɪk/ adj.

of the artificial part of the body 假肢的；人造的

poignant /ˈpɔɪnjənt/ *adj.*

having a strong effect on your feelings, especially in a way that makes you feel sad 悲惨的；酸楚的

consecutive /kənˈsekjətɪv/ *adj.*

following one after another in a series, without interruption 连续不断的

bonkers /ˈbɒŋkərz/ *adj.*

completely crazy and silly 疯狂；愚蠢透顶

endorsement /ɪnˈdɔːrsmənt/ *n.*

a statement made in an advertisement, usually by sb. famous or important, saying that they use and like a particular product 宣传；代言

history in the making

the process of becoming records in history 将载入史册

wring sth. from sb.

to obtain sth. from sb. with difficulty, especially by putting pressure on them 从……处费力弄到

cash in on sth.

to gain an advantage for yourself from a situation, especially in a way that other people think is wrong or immoral 从中牟利；捞好处

Reading Comprehension Questions

1. We learn from the first two paragraphs that the author's attitude towards the Olympics is one of _____.
   (A) approval   (B) cynicism
   (C) skepticism   (D) indifference

2. What can be learned about Gabby Douglas? _____
   (A) She is a 16-year-old black girl.

(B) She fulfilled her dream in cornfields.

(C) She knew she did not have to train in Iowa.

(D) She did not get along with her coach in Virginia.

3. Which of the following is true according to the text? _____

   (A) Sarah Attar won a gold medal.

   (B) Saudi Arabia sent one female athlete to the Olympics.

   (C) Kirani James made it possible for Oscar Pistorius to win the gold.

   (D) Phelps is the first man to collect more than 18 Olympian gold metals.

4. What was most important to May-Treanor and Walsh Jennings? _____

   (A) Medals. (B) Their friendship.

   (C) Their amazing adventure. (D) The journey off the court together.

5. Missy Franklin has decided to preserve her amateur status because _____.

   (A) she wants money and fame

   (B) she finds joy in defeating her rivals

   (C) she has something to teach others

   (D) she enjoys bringing excitement to her campus

(选文:任爱军;注释:许振宇)

3. We Still Need Information Stored in Our Heads Not "in the Cloud"[1]

By Annie Murphy Paul[2]

Computer are great for information that won't change, but a brain is better at connecting facts with other facts and acquiring layers of meaning

1   Is technology making us stupid — or smarter than we've ever been? Author Nicholas G. Carr[3] memorably made the case for the former in his 2010 book *The Shallows: What the Internet Is Doing to Our Brains*. This fall we'll have a rejoinder of sorts from writer Clive Thompson[4], with his book *Smarter Than You Think: How Technology Is Changing Our Minds for the Better*.

2   ① My own take: technology can make us smarter or more stupid, and we need to develop a set of principles to guide our everyday behavior and make sure that tech is improving and not impeding our mental processes. One of the big questions being debated today is, what kind of information do we need to have stored in our heads, and what kind can we leave "in the cloud", to be accessed as necessary?

3   In 2005, researchers at the University of Connecticut asked a group of seventh-graders to read a website full of information about the Pacific Northwest tree octopus, or *Octopus paxarbolis*. ② The Web page described the creature's mating rituals, preferred diet and leafy habitat in precise detail. Applying an analytical model they'd learned, the students evaluated the trustworthiness of the site and the information it offered.

4   Their judgment? The tree octopus was legit. All but one of the pupils rated the website as "very credible". The headline of the university's press release read, "Researchers Find Kids Need Better Online Academic Skills," and

it quoted Don Leu, professor of education at the University of Connecticut and co-director of its New Literacies Research Lab, lamenting that classroom instruction in online reading is "woefully lacking".

5   ③ There's something wrong with this picture, and it's not just that the arboreal octopus is, of course, a fiction, presented by Leu and his colleagues to probe their subjects' Internet savvy. The other fable here is the notion that the main thing these kids need — what all our kids really need — is to learn online skills in school. It would seem clear that what Leu's seventh-graders really require is knowledge: some basic familiarity with the biology of sea-dwelling creatures that would have tipped them off that the website was a whopper (say, when it explained that the tree octopus's natural predator is the sasquatch).

6   ④ But that's not how an increasingly powerful faction within education sees the matter. They are the champions of "new literacies" — or "21st century skills" or "digital literacy[5]" or a number of other faddish-sounding concepts. In their view, skills trump knowledge, developing "literacies" is more important than learning mere content, and all facts are now Google-able and therefore unworthy of committing to memory. But even the most sophisticated digital-literacy skills won't help students and workers navigate the world if they don't have a broad base of knowledge about how the world actually operates. "When we fill our classrooms with technology and emphasize these new 'literacies', we feel like we're reinventing schools to be more relevant," says Robert Pondiscio, executive director of the nonprofit organization CitizenshipFirst (and a former fifth-grade teacher). "But if you focus on the delivery mechanism and not the content, you're doing kids a disservice."

7   Indeed, evidence from cognitive science challenges the notion that skills can exist independent of factual knowledge. Dan Willingham, a professor of psychology at the University of Virginia, is a leading expert on how students learn. "Data from the last thirty years leads to a conclusion that is not scientifically challengeable: thinking well requires knowing facts, and that's true not only because you need something to think about," Willingham has

written. "The very processes that teachers care about most — critical thinking[6] processes such as reasoning and problem solving — are intimately intertwined with factual knowledge that is stored in long-term memory (not just found in the environment)."

8 ⑤ In other words, just because you can Google the date of Black Tuesday[7] doesn't mean you understand why the Great Depression[8] happened or how it compares to our recent economic slump. There is no doubt that the students of today, and the workers of tomorrow, will need to innovate, collaborate and evaluate, to name three of the "21st century skills" so dear to digital-literacy enthusiasts. But such skills can't be separated from the knowledge that gives rise to them. To innovate, you have to know what came before. To collaborate, you have to contribute knowledge to the joint venture. And to evaluate, you have to compare new information against knowledge you've already mastered.

9 So here's a principle for thinking in a digital world, in two parts:

10 **First, acquire a base of fact knowledge in any domain in which you want to perform well.**

11 This base supplies the essential foundation for building skills, and it can't be outsourced to a search engine.

12 **Second, take advantage of computers' invariant memory and also the brain's elaborative memory.**

13 Computers are great when you want to store information that shouldn't change — say, the date and time of that appointment next week. A computer (unlike your brain, or mine) won't misremember the time of the appointment as 3 p.m. instead of 2 p.m. But brains are the superior choice when you want information to change, in interesting and useful ways: to connect up with other facts and ideas, to acquire successive layers of meaning, to steep for a while in your accumulated knowledge and experience and so produce a richer mental brew.

(From *Time*, June 21, 2013)

Notes

[1] **The Cloud**: A network of remote servers hosted on the Internet and used to store, manage, and process data in place of local servers or personal computers.

[2] **Annie Murphy Paul**: A book author, magazine journalist, consultant and speaker who helps people understand how we learn and how we can do it better.

[3] **Nicholas G. Carr** (1959-): An American writer who has published books and articles on technology, business, and culture. His book *The Shallows: What the Internet Is Doing to Our Brains* was a finalist for the 2011 Pulitzer Prize in General Nonfiction.

[4] **Clive Thompson** (1968-): A Canadian freelance journalist, blogger and science and technology writer. He is a longtime contributing writer for the *New York Times* Magazine and a columnist for *Wired*. Thompson is one of the most prominent technology writers, respected for doing deeply-reported, long-form magazine stories that get beyond headlines and harness the insights of science, literature, history and philosophy. He specializes in writing not merely on the inventors of technologies, but about how everyday people use them—often quite unpredictably.

[5] **Digital Literacy**: The knowledge, skills, and behaviors used in a broad range of digital devices such as smartphones, tablets, laptops and desktop PCs, all of which are seen as network rather than computing devices.

[6] **Critical Thinking**: The objective analysis and evaluation of an issue in order to form a judgement.

[7] **Black Tuesday**: October 29, 1929. The Wall Street Crash of 1929, also known as Black Tuesday. On this date, share prices on the New York Stock Exchange completely collapsed, becoming a pivotal factor in the emergence of the Great Depression.

Words and Phrases

rejoinder /rɪˈdʒɔɪndə(r)/ n.

a reply, especially a sharp or witty one 回答

impede /ɪmˈpiːd/ v.

to interfere with the movement, progress, or development of something or somebody 阻碍

legit /lɪˈdʒɪt/

abbreviation of legitimate; conforming to the rules; legal 合法的

lament /ləˈment/ v.

express regret or disappointment about something 悲叹

woefully /ˈwəʊfəlɪ/ adv.

in a way that shows one feels sad 可怜地

arboreal /ɑːˈbɔːrɪəl/ adj.

living in trees 栖息在树上的

whopper /ˈwɒpə(r)/ n.

a gross or blatant lie 漫天大谎

savvy /ˈsævɪ/ n.

shrewdness and practical knowledge; the ability to make good judgements 悟性；理解能力

disservice /dɪsˈsɜːvɪs/ n.

a harmful action 危害；伤害

trump /trʌmp/ v.

surpass (something) by saying or doing something better 超过

outsource /ˈaʊtsɔːs/ v.

contract (work) out 外包

intertwine /ˌɪntəˈtwaɪn/ v.

connect or link (two or more things) closely 密切关联

Google /ˈɡuːɡl/ v.

search for information about (someone or something) on the Internet using the search engine Google　用谷歌搜索引擎搜索

tip someone off

informal give someone information in a discreet or confidential way　向某人透露消息

give rise to

cause to happen　使发生

Suggested Topics for Writing

1. Some people think technology is making us stupid while others believe we are smarter because of technology. What is your idea about the issue? Please give specific reasons or examples to support your idea.

2. Bill Gates once said: "Digital tools magnify the abilities that make us unique in the world: the ability to think, the ability to articulate our thoughts, the ability to work together to act on those thoughts." Please make some comment on his statement with a view to "We Still Need Information Stored in Our Heads Not 'in the Cloud'".

(选文:徐守平;注释:斯骏)

Key to Comprehension Questions

Unit One　New Trends

1. "Mystery Meat" Takes on a Whole New Meaning
   BCBCC
2. Friends? Who Needs Them
   BDDDD

Unit Two　Individual Growth

1. The Essence of Charm
   CADCD
2. Average Is Over
   DBDAA

Unit Three　Youth Today

1. How Those Spoiled Millennials Will Make the Workplace Better for Everyone
   ADBAB

Unit Four　Social Concerns

1. The Price of Marriage in China
   ABDAC

2. Will There Be Any Nature Left?
CACDC

Unit Five Business and Market

1. Things Go Better with Quark?
BDACD
2. What Is a Bank?
CDDBA

Unit Six Technology Development

1. Human Gait Could Soon Power Portable Electronics
DBACD
2. How Solar Can Save India's Farmers
CBDAC

Unit Seven Medical World

1. Why We Should Study Cancer Like We Study Ecosystems
CCDAB
2. Three Ways Video Games Can Improve Health Care
ACCBC

Unit Eight Coping Strategies

1. Water Damage
BBCAA

Unit Nine Surviving Skills

1. Survival of the Biggest

DCACA

Unit Ten Education Issues

1. The Trouble with Online Education
   CDACD

Unit Eleven Culture Studies

1. *Lost in Thailand*: Did China's Comedy Hit Get Lost in Translation?
   CADAB

Unit Twelve New Insight

1. Why Waiting Is Torture
   DCBAC

Unit Thirteen Personality and Character

1. The Ungrateful President
   DABDA
2. The Five Images of Love
   BBCDD

Unit Fourteen New Horizon

1. What If Women Ruled the World?
   CABCB
2. The Soul of the Olympics
   AADBD